ALASKA GEOGRAPHIC

Mammals of Alaska

Published by
The Alaska Geographic Society · Anchorage, Alaska

COVER: *Dall sheep. (Harry M. Walker)*

PREVIOUS PAGE: *Arctic ground squirrel. (Charles Rushing)*

LIBRARY OF CONGRESS CATALOGING-IN-PUBLICATION DATA

Mammals of Alaska : a comprehensive guide from the publishers of Alaska geographic.
    p.   cm. -- (Alaska geographic guides)
    Includes bibliographical references (p.   ) and index.
    ISBN 1-56661-034-6 (pbk.)
    1. Mammals--Alaska.   I. Alaska geographic.   II. Series.
QL719.A4M35   1996
599.09798--dc20   96-44185
                                    CIP

DESIGN BY: Kathy Doogan

COLOR SEPARATIONS BY: Graphic Chromatics

The Alaska Geographic Society
P.O. Box 93370 • Anchorage, AK 99509-3370

PRINTED IN KOREA

Contents

Acknowledgements

ALASKA GEOGRAPHIC® readers have asked from time to time for a replacement for the original *ALASKA GEOGRAPHIC®* monograph, *Alaska Mammals* (Vol. 8, No. 2). And certainly a series of guidebooks on the state is hardly complete without a guide to the fascinating mammals that make up part of the Alaska mystique.

To compile such a guide required the cooperation of biologists, naturalists and wildlife specialists both private and public. *ALASKA GEOGRAPHIC®* is grateful for assistance and text review from the following scientists:

Jim Baichtal, U.S. Forest Service, U.S. Department of Agriculture; Beth Matthews, National Park Service, U.S. Department of the Interior; Jon R. Nickles, U.S. Fish and Wildlife Service, U.S. Department of the Interior;

Porcupine. (George Wuerthner)

Red fox, cross phase. (Lon E. Lauber)

Linda Shaw, National Marine Fisheries Service, U.S. Department of Commerce.

Ed Crain, Kathy Frost, Lloyd Lowry, Steve Peterson, Ted Spraker and Nancy Tankersley of the Alaska Department of Fish and Game.

Kate Wynne, Sea Grant Marine Advisory Program; David R. Klein, Terry Bowyer and Bill Hauer of the Institute of Arctic Biology, University of Alaska Fairbanks; and Joe Cook, University of Alaska Museum. ■

Introduction

For many, Alaska's wildlife is the Great Land's major attraction. Sharing billing with the bears, moose, caribou, sheep and goats are species ranging from the mythical muskox and bowhead whale to tiny mammals that go about their business with scarcely a second look from the state's more prominent species, including man.

This edition of *Mammals of Alaska* seeks to include all species listed for the state as of January 1996. But as with most lists, entries come and go based on current scientific thinking. New species have appeared on the Alaska roster just since *ALASKA GEOGRAPHIC®* staff began this project. And animals themselves move, expanding their range to gain a toehold in the state or simply straying from their home area and ending up in Alaska. For instance, confirmation of the hooded seal in Alaska comes from one specimen that was found on the North Slope in 1976. Risso's dolphins and long-finned pilot whales are likely in Alaska's waters from time to time but they normally occur farther south.

Other species make the list as feral animals that have escaped from their captors and found the Great Land to their liking. For example, in 1995 Ketchikan residents reported feral rabbits on Betton Island in

Least weasel. (D. Pattie, American Society of Mammalogists)

Gray wolves. (Ernest Manewal)

Clover Pass. The European or domestic rabbit (*Oryctolagus cuniculus*) is now on the Alaska mammals list.

The species are presented alphabetically, with the hope that this will help readers find the animals of their interest more quickly. Whenever possible, the staff has included a photo of the species. For some of the smaller mammals, this has resulted at times in inclusion of a photo representative of the genus. A glossary contains some of the more common scientific terms associated with Alaska's mammals. These terms appear in **bold type** at their first occurrence within the text.

The *ALASKA GEOGRAPHIC*® staff hope this guide helps Alaska's wildlife watchers go forth better armed in their search for glimpses into the world of mammals in the Great Land. ■

Bats
Vespertilionidae Family

Description: Even though bats make up about one-fifth of all mammal species, Alaska has only six species of these, the only flying mammals. The Vespertilionidae or evening bats in Alaska separate into four *Myotis* species, which are small and dark brown, and two other species. The *Myotis* bats have erratic flight patterns and weigh about 33/100 of an ounce. The little brown bat, most common of the state's bat species, is about 2 inches long with a 6-inch wingspan. Precise identification among the four species, *Myotis lucifugus* (little brown bat), *Myotis volans* (long-legged bat), *Myotis keenii* (Keen's bat) and *Myotis californicus* (California bat), is difficult and requires an expert.

Lasionycteris noctivagans (silver-haired bat) and *Eptesicus fuscus* (big brown bat) are Alaska's other two bat species. The back of the silver-haired bat has white-tipped hairs over a basically dark coat. This species weighs 38/100 of an ounce and has a wingspan from 8 to 12 inches.

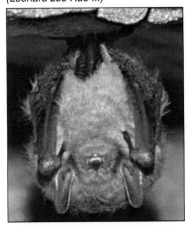
(Leonard Lee Rue III)

The big brown bat is larger still, weighing 63/100 of an ounce with a wingspan of 13 inches to 15 1/2 inches. Its slower, more direct flight and larger size distinguish it from Alaska's other bats.

Range: The wintering area of Alaska's bats is unknown. Scientists do know that as soon as temperatures drop to 33 degrees to 35 degrees, bats enter caves and either go into hibernation or become torpid. In lower elevation caves, bats go far enough back in the cave to cross the boundary between freezing and non-freezing air, or they find a pocket of high humidity within the cave that keeps them from losing too much body moisture during cold periods. Under these conditions the bats are torpid and not true hibernators. Even during the dead of winter, if temperatures rise above freezing, the bats will wake and feed on moss and flying insects.

Little Brown Bat:	Most widely distributed of Alaska's bats, generally in Southeast, Southcentral including Kodiak, north into the Interior.
Long-legged Bat:	Primarily Southeast.
Keen's Bat:	Three specimens from Southeast.
Silver-haired Bat:	Two specimens from Southeast.
Big Brown Bat:	One record from Delta in the Interior.
California Bat:	Southeast. Specimens found on Prince of Wales and Long islands.

Food: Insects. They find their prey on night flights with sophisticated echolocation, sending out high-pitched squeaks that bounce off prey or obstacles in their flight path.

Life History: Little brown bats mate in fall, store the sperm in the female's uterus and delay development of the embryo until May. One or two naked, blind young are born in June to each pregnant female. A few adults tend the newborn nursing colony for about a month, at which time the youngsters strike out on their own.

Myotis bats seem to roost in colonies in abandoned buildings or mine tunnels. They have been found roosting singly in trees or rock crevices. Silver-haired and big brown bats are more solitary in feeding and roosting. Silver-haired have been spotted in trees, big browns in hollow trees, abandoned buildings and caves.

Bats are not the bad guys they are sometimes made out to be. They can get into chimneys or attics, but sealing the entrances curtails that problem. And since 500 little brown bats can eat half a million mosquitoes in a night, they definitely do their part to control the hordes of mosquitoes that can plague an Alaska outing.

Scientists have documented bats living 20 years in the wild. ■

Black Bear

Ursus americanus

(Harry M. Walker)

Description: Black bears vary in color. Usually they are jet black with a buff muzzle and often a small white chest patch; sometimes they are brown. Rarely they are smoky-blue, blue-gray or smoky-gray, the result of recessive genes. Bears with the blue-gray coloration, commonly called glacier bears, are found usually along the Gulf of Alaska coast between Yakutat and Glacier Bay. Another rare color phase is the white or cream-colored black bear that lives on British Columbia's Kermode Island and vicinity.

Black bears, especially the brown color phase, may be confused with brown/grizzlies. A large black bear may be bigger than a small grizzly, although normally grizzlies are much larger. Black bears have a smaller, more pointed head, with a straight profile; grizzlies have a dish-shaped face, with a larger, blunter, heavier and round-appearing head. Grizzlies also sport a distinct shoulder hump absent in black bears. Blacks have short, narrow, dark and markedly curved front claws; grizzlies have long, broad, slightly curved and commonly light-colored front claws.

Average adult males stand 29 inches high at the shoulder and reach 60 inches from nose to tail. They weigh from 180 to 200 pounds in spring. Females are usually about 20 percent smaller. Both sexes weigh 20 to 30 percent more in fall than in spring.

Range: Black bears inhabit most of forested Alaska. They are seldom found north of the Brooks Range, on the western Seward Peninsula, on the Yukon-Kuskokwim delta or the Alaska Peninsula south of the Alagnak River. They do not occur on the Kodiak archipelago or on large islands in Southeast north of Frederick Sound.

Food: Black bears are omnivorous, although most of the time they are vegetarians because meat and fish are less readily available. During spring, they feed on early growing vegetation, including grasses and sedges. They eat carrion and young deer and moose, and scavenge garbage dumps when readily available or when natural food is scarce. As summer progresses, coastal bears gather at salmon streams during fish runs. Otherwise they eat primarily berries and insects. Males will occasionally kill cubs if bear density is high.

Life History: Breeding takes place from June through July. Implantation of the fertilized egg occurs when the female enters her den in the fall, but development of the egg doesn't begin for some time. The 8- to 10-ounce cubs, usually two, are born in winter or early spring. Cubs are precocious after they leave the den and are weaned by September. The family enters winter sleep together, and doesn't break up until the following spring when the female breeds again. Females living in good habitat typically breed every other year, every third year in more marginal areas. Both sexes mature when they are about age 3 1/2, although some females may not breed until they are 5 or 6.

When temperatures drop and food becomes scarce, black bears enter their den to sleep through the winter. Their body temperature drops and their metabolic rate slows. They usually do not leave their den until spring, although individuals in southern areas may emerge from their den off and on throughout the winter. Animals farther north may sleep for seven to eight months.

A female black bear recently captured in the Petersburg area was 27 years old. ∎

Brown/Grizzly Bear
Ursus arctos

Description: The color of brown/grizzly bears varies from area to area. Some bears are black with silver-tipped hairs; others are blond. Most are some shade of brown or gray-brown, and bears with a blond body and dark brown legs are common. Males tend to be darker than females, and cubs commonly sport a white collar through their first summer.

Brown/grizzly bears vary in size, depending on gender, age, time of year and geographic location. Alaskans customarily refer to coastal bears as brown bears or brownies and interior bears as grizzlies. Brownies are usually about one-third larger than grizzlies.

Alaska's brown bears are the largest living carnivorous land mammals. Polar bears grow as large, perhaps larger, but they are not considered land-dwelling mammals. Unusually large brownies may grow to between 8 and 9 feet, stand more than 4 feet high at the shoulders and weigh about 1,500 pounds. Typically, however, they weigh between 500 and 900 pounds. Mature females normally weigh about half as much as equivalent-aged males in the same area. Brown/grizzlies weigh 20 to 30 percent more in fall than in spring throughout their range.

Most scientists think that the brown/grizzly of North America and the European brown bear are the same species, *Ursus arctos horribilis*. Brownies from the Kodiak island group are reproductively isolated, with distinctive skull features, and are considered a separate subspecies, *Ursus arctos middendorffi*.

Range: Brown/grizzlies range throughout the state except for islands south of Frederick Sound in Southeast and in the Aleutians beyond Unimak Island.

Food: A varied diet, depending on season and area, sustains Alaska's brown/grizzly population. In spring, the bears feed mainly on grasses and early herbaceous plants. In summer and fall, fruit, berries and shrubs supplement the grasses.

While meat and fish are not a big part of a bear's diet, except when salmon are running in summer and early fall, brown/grizzlies will eat whatever they can catch. Marmots, squirrels and mice, moose, caribou, deer, insect larvae, carrion and other bears will be eaten if the chance presents itself.

Life History: Brown/grizzlies reach sexual maturity at different ages, depending on their location. On Kodiak Island and the Alaska Peninsula, both sexes reach maturity at age 3 1/2 to 6 1/2. In the eastern Brooks Range, they become mature at 6 1/2 to 12 1/2.

Breeding occurs from May through July. The 8- to 10-ounce hairless cubs are born in January or February, following a gestation period of about 245 days, which includes a relatively long term of delayed implantation when the fertilized egg lies nearly dormant. Implantation occurs in October or November. Litter size varies from one to four, with two the most common. Females inhabiting areas with more nutritious food supplies produce the larger litters.

(Patrick J. Endres)

The frequency of breeding also depends on food supply. The interval between cub production in the northern Brooks Range is about four years, on the Alaska Peninsula three years. Most bears nurse their cubs for one or two summers, some for three. Then the family breaks up, and the sow breeds again.

Brown/grizzlies will adopt orphaned cubs. Observers have reported mixed-age litters of yearlings and cubs-of-the-year, and of seeing a sow with cubs of different sizes that are obviously of different ages.

Brown/grizzlies enter a dormant period each winter when they den, lower their body temperature and metabolic rate and eliminate their need for food and water. As with black bears, animals in colder environments remain in their dens longer.

Although at least one male has been recorded living to age 34 in the wild, 22 years is about average for males, slightly more for females. ■

Polar Bear
Ursus maritimus

Description: Dark-colored eyes, nose and lips are the only exception to the overall white appearance of the polar bear, whose coat may look yellowish, or brownish-white in summer. Younger bears often appear whiter because the coat of adults is stained by fat from their prey, marine mammals.

(Kathy Frost, ADF&G)

A polar bear has a long neck, and proportionately small head with small ears. Large, strong claws protrude from well-furred feet. They are at home in water, and reports exist of swimming bears seen at least 50 miles from the nearest ice or land. In the water, polar bears propel themselves with their front paws and trail their rear paws.

Males average 8 1/2 feet and 900 pounds but have been recorded at 1,500 pounds or more; females average 6 1/2 feet and 500 pounds.

Range: Polar bears inhabit the arctic ice pack and are more numerous near its southern edge. When they do come on shore, they usually stay near the coast, although they have been recorded as much as 100 miles inland.

Off western Alaska, these bears gradually move northward in spring through Bering Strait and into the Chukchi Sea ahead of the receding ice pack. They spend the summer on the ice, hunting largely along its edge, which may vary from 10 to 200 miles off Alaska's north coast. Bears move south

(Scott L. Schliebe, USFWS)

again in the fall as the ice advances, and are frequently found as far south as St. Lawrence Island.

Food: Their diet consists mainly of ringed and bearded seals, which they catch when seals come to breathing holes in winter, or stalk when seals are resting on the ice in summer. Polar bears also eat walrus, stranded whales, birds, fish and some vegetation. Boars will kill and eat polar bear cubs.

Life History: Solitary except for females with young and when gathered around a whale or walrus carcass, polar bears breed in late March, April and May. Males follow the tracks of females across the ice, mate, then move on. In October, pregnant females seek dens, usually in cold, stable areas, sometimes as much as 30 miles inland, along the coast or on shorefast or drifting ice.

After delayed implantation, young are born, usually in December. Generally a sow bears two cubs weighing about a pound each. The sow remains in the den with the cubs until March or April when the cubs have gained 14 pounds or so.

Cubs stay with the sow for another two years. Females breed again when they separate from their young, so most sows off Alaska's coast produce a litter every third year.

Scientists estimate polar bears live 25 to 30 years. ■

Beaver

Castor canadensis

Description: Beaver are the largest of North American
rodents. They have thick brown fur that consists of long
guard hairs and dense underfur; a robust body; broad, flat,
scaly tail; short ears and webbed hind feet. Their tail, about
10 inches long and 6 inches wide, acts as a rudder when they
swim. An individual slaps its tail against the water to
communicate with other beavers, sometimes to signal danger
but also to express other emotions. The tail also aids balance
when a beaver stands on its hind legs to cut down a tree.
Castor glands near the tail produce an odorous, oily
substance that attracts other beaver.

Beaver continue to grow throughout their life. They can
reach 3 or 4 feet, including tail, and weigh 40 to 70 pounds,
although individuals weighing
100 pounds have been recorded.

(Michael Mauro)

Range: Beaver are distributed throughout most of the forested Alaska mainland from the Brooks Range south to the middle of the Alaska Peninsula and into Southeast. They were introduced to the Kodiak area in 1925 and are now well-established on some islands in that group.

Food: Beaver eat a variety of plants including leaves and bark of deciduous trees and shrubs, and roots and stems of aquatic vegetation and sedges. They also feed on conifers, such as spruce. Beaver can harvest vegetation while underwater by pressing their lower lip behind their front teeth to prevent water from entering their mouth.

Life History: Beaver breed in January or February. Following a gestation period of about 100 days, the female bears a litter that averages four. About the time the litter arrives, 2-year-olds are driven off to form new colonies elsewhere.

Depending on how thick the ice may get in winter, beaver generally require at least 2 or 3 feet of water year-round to survive. They construct dams to create the ponds in which they build their houses and dig canals through which they swim and float their harvest of trees and large branches. Beaver will harvest a tree 150 feet tall and 5 feet across. Larger trees are stripped of their bark, which the beaver eat. Smaller trees are cut into manageable size and maneuvered to reinforce the dam or lodge. Many dams are 10 to 15 feet in height and 20 feet across at the base. Beaver houses have underwater entrances; anchored in the mud nearby is their winter food supply of cut tree branches. When winter comes and the pond freezes over, beaver houses, built partly of mud, also freeze, and virtually no predator can break through. A beaver house is big enough for parents and litters of two years: perhaps 10 beavers. Such a room, 4 or 5 feet across and perhaps 3 feet high, is large enough for a man.

Beaver live 10 to 12 years in the wild and have survived to 19 in captivity. ◼

American Bison
Bison bison

Description: American bison are large, predominantly brown bovines with long, shaggy hair; short, curved horns; a high hump at the shoulder; and long hair on the head and chin that is especially heavy on males.

The largest land mammal native to North America, bison bulls may weigh more than 1 ton, stand 6 feet at the shoulder and grow to 10 feet long; cows weigh 800 to 1,200 pounds.

Range: The core herd grazes near Delta Junction in the Tanana Valley about 100 miles southeast of Fairbanks. Offshoots of this herd roam near Farewell in the Interior,

(Tom Soucek)

and at Nabesna and Chitina in the Copper River Basin. At times, a few private herds have grazed confined areas in the Interior, Southcentral and Southwest.

Food: Although they do eat some shrubs, bison are predominantly grazers; the lack of abundant grass in winter limits their numbers in Alaska. Preferred foods include grasses, sedges, forbs, legumes and willow twigs.

Life History: Alaska's modern bison descend from about 20 animals transplanted to the territory in 1928 from Montana. The transplant reintroduced a species that last lived in Alaska about 500 years ago.

Breeding occurs from mid-June through September, with the peak in August. Bulls ages 6 to 14 do most of the breeding. Males are sexually mature at age 2 or 3, but older bulls prevent young ones from breeding. Cows are apparently bred by only one bull, although one bull may breed many cows.

Females are sexually mature at age 2, but drop their first calf at age 3 or 4. Most cows bear a single calf twice in three years.

Peak calving occurs in May and June after a gestation period of about nine months. Calves are weaned at 7 to 8 months.

While most images of bison depict great herds thundering across the plains, Alaska bison migrate in small groups. They move to secluded calving grounds early in the spring, and spend the summer and fall working their way to wintering grounds. Although they may appear ungainly, bison display speed, endurance and agility when necessary. A bull from the Delta herd was observed jumping a 7-foot log fence from a standing start.

Bison have a relatively long life compared to other hoofed mammals in Alaska. A tagged bull killed in the Copper River Basin was more than 20 years old. ■

Caribou
Rangifer tarandus

Description: In late fall, caribou are clove-brown with a white neck and rump, and often with a white flank stripe. They have lighter hair underneath and, as the seasons pass, their coat lightens because of wear that exposes the underhair and because of bleaching by the sun.

Caribou are the only deer in which both sexes grow antlers, large and massive on bulls, much shorter and usually more slender and irregular on cows. Mature bulls may grow antlers about 4 feet from base to tip.

Caribou have large, concave hooves that splay to support them on snow, ice, soft tundra and gravel, and serve as paddles when they swim. Hollow hair cells trap air, enabling caribou to swim with their back high out of the water.

Adult bulls weigh 350 to 600 pounds in the fall, although weights of 700 pounds have been recorded for caribou introduced to Adak Island in the Aleutians. Mature cows average 175 to 225 pounds. Caribou inhabiting the southern part of their range usually grow larger than do those farther north.

Large herds of reindeer, the domesticated form of caribou, roam parts of western Alaska. Usually reindeer are smaller than their wild relatives and, by law, only Natives can own reindeer in Alaska.

Range: At one time or another, caribou have inhabited almost the entire state except for Southeast and most offshore islands. Alaska has about 31 distinct caribou herds with some overlapping of ranges. Some scientists have maintained that there really is only one caribou herd in Alaska, with various segments settling in specific areas for varying amounts of time.

Currently, caribou range throughout the state except for

(Patrick J. Endres)

most of the Yukon River
valley, the outer Seward
Peninsula, the Yukon-Kuskokwim delta, outer Kenai
Peninsula, Prince William Sound, Southeast and many but
not all Aleutian Islands.

Food: Like most herd animals, caribou must keep moving
to find adequate food. This distributes feeding pressure and
lessens overgrazing. In summer caribou eat a variety of
plants, favoring grasses, sedges, succulents and willow and
dwarf birch leaves. When autumn frost kills plants and
foliage, caribou switch to lichens and dried sedges. In spring,
caribou look for the new growth of grasses, sedges and other
plants.

Life History: Social creatures, caribou are found most often
in groups of from a few to tens of thousands. They travel

incessantly, moving among calving grounds, summer and winter range and breeding and fall range. Insects also cause herds to move and scatter, each animal seeking relief in water or on snow patches from mosquitoes, warble flies and nose flies.

Caribou are polygamous. Bulls mature sexually at 16 to 28 months; their antlers become increasingly larger until individuals reach their prime at ages 4 to 5 years. Cows are sexually mature at 28 months, although a few breed at 18 months, and some not until 40 months.

They produce a single reddish-brown calf, weighing from 11 to 20 pounds. Newborns can travel with their mother within an hour of birth and within a few days they can run and swim with the herd.

When snows fall in September, caribou move to lower elevations, where males and females join in mixed bands, and males begin shedding antler velvet, signaling the onset of the breeding cycle. Breeding peaks in mid-October as the herd moves toward winter range.

Since caribou require relatively undisturbed tundra and northern forest, habitat loss through natural and man-caused disruptions invariably leads to lowered numbers. Calving range is critical to the herd's existence; migration routes between ranges may be equally important.

Wild caribou are known to have lived 15 years, although the average is more like 4 and 1/2 years. Captive animals have lived to more than 20 years. ■

Coyote
Canis latrans

Description: Coyotes vary in color in different parts of their range, but generally they are coarsely grizzled, buff-gray and black. The bushy tail is usually blackish above, pale buff underneath with a black tip.

Coyotes resemble small, slender wolves. They reach 42 to 50 inches from nose to tail tip, and stand 24 inches high at the shoulder. Coyotes average 22 to 33 pounds, about one-third the weight of wolves.

Range: Coyotes are found as far west as the Alaska Peninsula and the north side of Bristol Bay, and as far north as the northern flank of the Brooks Range. They are less common in areas with substantial wolf populations.

Food: Being great opportunists, coyotes eat anything that crosses their path and provides protein. The young of big game, snowshoe hares, ground squirrels, mice, waterfowl, eggs, carrion and berries have at one time or another sustained coyotes. In Alaska they also prey on Dall sheep, marmots, muskrats, fish and insects. Coyotes have been known to work cooperatively to tackle larger prey, and when hunting rodents, they adopt a technique used by foxes, pouncing in a high arc to come straight down on the rodents, often trapping them under vegetation.

Life History: Females become sexually mature during their second winter and usually produce one litter per year. Breeding occurs from February to March, with litters — usually of five to seven but sometimes more — born after about a 60-day gestation period. Pups are born in a den dug into a hillside or steep bank. Sometimes dens are enlarged marmot or squirrel burrows.

(Chlaus Lotscher)

Both parents care for the young, assisted by coyotes born in previous years. The pups go from eating milk to regurgitated food. They are weaned at 5 to 7 weeks. At about 3 months they begin to hunt for themselves.

A coyote's average life span is 10 to 12 years in the wild.

Sitka Black-tailed Deer

Odocoileus hemionus sitkensis

(Harry M. Walker)

Description: The reddish-brown summer coat is replaced by a dark gray or blue-gray coat in winter. The jet-black top of the deer's tail contrasts with its white bottom. Both sexes have dark foreheads that shade to light gray around the nose of older animals.

Antlers, found only on bucks, are dark brown with typical black-tailed branching: On each side of the head the main beam branches into a Y; on larger deer each arm of the Y may fork again. Fully developed antlers have five points, including the eye guard, on each side. Sitka deer have small antlers compared with Columbian black-tailed deer living farther south. Largest antlers normally occur on bucks age 4 and 5.

Sitka black-tailed deer, smallest of the black-tailed group, have a stockier build and shorter face than other blacktails. In October, bucks average about 120 pounds, does about 80 pounds. They stand 40 to 42 inches at the shoulder and reach 90 to 100 inches from nose to tip of tail.

Range: Black-tailed deer, a coastal form of mule deer, inhabit British Columbia, Washington, Oregon and northern California. Sitka black-tailed deer are native to Southeast Alaska and to northcoastal British Columbia.

Individuals have been transplanted successfully to Kodiak and Afognak islands, to the mainland and all major islands of Prince William Sound and to the Yakutat area.

Food: In spring, deer in Southeast first feed on beach rye, goose tongue, sedges and skunk cabbage. As spring progresses, deer eat new growth of blueberry and salmonberry. In June, they head toward alpine areas, feeding on emerging growth as the snow retreats. They live for a time in densely forested areas interspersed with muskeg openings where diet staples include skunk cabbage, marsh marigold, ground dogwood, trailing bramble and goldthread.

Alpine areas from 2,000 to 3,500 feet in elevation are the most important summer range. Deer usually reach this area in July, although yearlings and does with fawns remain at lower elevations all summer.

Mountain hemlock, salmonberry, dwarf alder and black currant supplement the most important alpine summer food, deer cabbage, which contains between 15 and 25 percent protein.

Fall weather pushes deer to lower elevations where they resume eating the same species they ate in the spring in addition to ground dogwood and trailing bramble. In winter and early spring, deer need mixed-age old-growth forest to find shelter and forage.

During extreme winters, deer eat almost any plant they can reach. When deep snows force deer onto tide-washed beaches, they eat seaweeds, usually kelp, which have little nutrition.

Life History: Rutting begins in late October and peaks about mid-November. Does first breed at age 2 and continue bearing young until they are 10 or 12. Does reach the height of their productivity between ages 5 and 10, when they typically have two fawns per season. Fawns, reddish-brown with a line of white spots along each side of the back and scattered white spots on both sides, are born in May and June, usually in the forest bordering lowland muskeg or beaches. Fawns weigh 6 to 8 pounds at birth.

Deer in Alaska spend most of their lives within a short distance of where they are born. Tagging has shown this repeatedly, and a 10-mile-to-12-mile move seems to be about the farthest deer travel from their home ground.

Besides human hunters, wolves are the only serious predators on deer, although black and brown bears kill some.

The average life span of Sitka black-tailed deer in Alaska is relatively short, with only about 10 percent of the population living longer than 5 years, although records indicate some individuals have reached age 10 or older. Because Sitka deer live in marginal habitat at the northern end of their range, their numbers may fluctuate dramatically depending on the severity of winters. ■

Pacific White-Sided Dolphin

Lagenorhynchus obliquidens

Description: A black back, striking light gray sides and a white belly mark the Pacific white-sided dolphin. A white stripe begins just behind the head, continues along the back to the dorsal fin, then widens and curves toward the anus. These dolphins frequently ride a ship's bow wave, at which time this stripe is clearly visible. Their large, sickle-shaped dorsal fin is black in front and gray in back.

Pacific white-sided dolphins reach more than 7 feet and weigh about 300 pounds.

This species and Dall's porpoises sport somewhat similar markings and sometimes travel together. To distinguish the two, note that the dolphins like to jump out of the water and can turn somersaults; Dall's porpoises seldom jump.

Range: This species ranges the North Pacific, including the Gulf of Alaska, Prince William Sound and Aleutian waters, and has been recorded as far south as Baja California. They are found primarily in offshore waters, although there are increasingly frequent sightings in Southeast's inside waters.

(John Hall)

Food: They eat small schooling fish and squid.

Life History: Little is known about their breeding, but they likely breed and calve in spring and summer, with a single calf about 3 feet long born after a 10- to 12-month gestation.

They may live to 45 years. ■

Elk or Wapiti
Cervus elaphus

Description: Elk have a grayish to brownish body with dark brown legs and neck, and a large, yellowish rump patch that is visible from some distance.

Only bulls have antlers, which in prime bulls are large and sweep back over the shoulder with daggerlike spikes that are light-tipped and point forward. Elk have antlers that tend to form two or three points at the end of each main stem, a feature called crowning.

Elk shed their antlers in late winter and grow new ones the following spring and summer. Velvet covers the soft, growing

(Tim Van Nest)

antlers. After the antlers harden in the fall, elk scrape off the velvet by rubbing the antlers against saplings.

Elk reach about 6 to 10 feet in length and stand 2 1/2 to 5 feet at the shoulder. Bull Roosevelt elk on Afognak Island have been weighed at more than 1,000 pounds dressed weight, which means at least 1,300 pounds live weight, about the same as young adult moose. Rocky Mountain elk are slightly smaller.

Range: Roosevelt elk inhabit Afognak and Raspberry islands north of Kodiak, and are expanding their territory in Southeast from Etolin to other islands. Individuals and small groups of elk have been spotted on neighboring islands and on the mainland. The Southeast population stems from a small herd of Roosevelt and Rocky Mountain elk that were transplanted to Etolin Island in 1987.

The Afognak and Raspberry herds developed from a 1928 transplant of eight elk calves captured on Washington state's Olympic Peninsula.

Food: Alaska's elk graze on grasses, sedges, fireweed and other herbaceous plants from late spring to early fall. As winter approaches, they switch to woody browse such as elderberry, highbush cranberry, willow and devil's club. Elk also eat fern roots, blueberry, salmonberry and mushrooms.

Life History: **Bugling** starts in late August and continues through mid-October, heralding the mating season, which peaks in late September. During the mating season, bulls and cows band together, with bulls scattered throughout the herd, actively breeding.

Calves, normally only one per pregnant cow, are born in late May and early June, usually in dense spruce forests hidden from predators. When a few days old, the calf, with its mother, rejoins the herd.

As summer progresses, the herd moves to alpine areas where feeding is better and winds keep down insects. By July, nursing calves begin feeding on succulent plants. In summer, bulls typically separate from the herd, but rejoin for mating. In late fall, the herd returns to lower elevations to spend the winter.

Elk seldom live more than 12 to 15 years in the wild. A captive animal lived for almost 27 years. ■

Arctic Fox
Alopex lagopus

Description: Arctic foxes come in two color phases, white and blue. In summer, white-phase foxes appear brown above and buff on the chest, flanks and belly. In winter, only the black nose and eyes contrast with the pure white coat. Blue-phase foxes appear gray in summer and lighter gray in winter.

Arctic foxes are small with a short face; low, rounded ears; a bushy tail and long, dense fur.

They grow to 43 inches in length, including a 15-inch tail, stand 9 to 12 inches at the shoulder and weigh 6 to 10 pounds, occasionally more.

Range: This species is found along the Arctic and Bering Sea coasts as far south as the Aleutian Islands. The white color phase predominates in the north and on St. Lawrence and Nunivak islands where the species occurs naturally. Arctic foxes have been introduced to the Pribilof and Aleutian islands where the blue color phase, favored by fox farmers, is more common.

Arctic fox, blue phase.
(Edward Steele)

Food: Predators and scavengers, arctic foxes feed on hares, rodents (especially lemmings), birds, eggs and a variety of carrion. They patrol beaches searching for food, and will eat almost any protein tossed up by the surf. They travel far out on the sea ice — one animal

Arctic fox, white phase.
(Ernest Manewal)

captured along the Russian coast was recaptured in Wainwright, Alaska. They will eat leftovers from polar bear and wolf kills. They take seabirds and are commonly found in rookeries, scampering among steep cliffs where they eat eggs, chicks and adult birds. Arctic foxes feed on spawning salmon and berries in fall.

Life History: Breeding occurs in March and April for this prolific species that reaches sexual maturity in its first year. After a 52-day gestation, a litter averaging seven is born in a den excavated in elevated, well-drained soil. Enlarged ground squirrel burrows are favored sites. Both color phases may appear in the same litter

After about a month, the pups play near the den's entrance while the parents bring home food. Pups compete intensely for food, and in times of prey scarcity, mortality is high. Pups are fully weaned by 1 1/2 months. By fall the youngsters can fend for themselves and the family breaks up.

Arctic foxes have an average life span of about 10 years. ∎

Red Fox
Vulpes vulpes

(Michael Mauro)

Description: The most common color for red foxes is a rich red-gold, with black legs and feet. Chest and underparts are usually white. Other color phases are pure black, silver (black with silver-tipped guard hairs), and cross (brownish-yellow, with a dark band across the shoulders and down the back). Two other variations, less common, are the samson fox (without guard hairs and with a woolly pelt) and a bastard fox (with a dark smoky coat midway between the normal red and black). Red foxes have a long bushy tail tipped with white. Their fur is long, full and soft.

This species reaches 3 to 4 feet in length, stands 16 to 18 inches at the shoulder and weighs 6 to 15 pounds or more.

Range: Red foxes occur throughout Alaska except for most areas of Prince William Sound and Southeast. In Southeast, they are relatively scarce but are found in the Taku and Stikine river valleys and on Douglas Island near Juneau. They are native to Kodiak Island and occur naturally as far west as Umnak Island in the Aleutians. Red foxes were introduced to other Aleutian Islands for farming; some of these foxes were later eradicated to allow introduction of arctic foxes. Where red fox and arctic fox ranges overlap, red fox are dominant and have been observed killing arctic foxes.

Food: Red foxes are omnivorous. They eat small mammals such as mice and hares, which seem to be their preferred prey, birds, eggs, plants, carrion; and in summer and fall, berries and insects.

Life History: Breeding occurs in February and March, with litters, usually of four pups, born 53 days later, normally in a den dug into the side of a well-drained hill. Records exist of litters with 12 pups, and all color phases may occur in one litter.

Pups are blind for their first eight or nine days. They remain in the den for the first three or four weeks, and continue to hunt from there for about three months. The mother teaches the pups to hunt during summer and early fall, after which the family breaks up and each individual goes its own way.

Red foxes live for about 10 years. ■

Mountain Goat
Oreamnos americanus

Description: White-haired mountain goats have a short body and humped shoulders. Their narrow head has a black muzzle, sharply pointed ears and a beard. Coarse guard hairs up to 7 inches long form heavy mats over the shoulders and hips. The coat grows to within 8 inches of each hoof, then stops abruptly.

Slender, black, back-curved horns grow 10 to 12 inches. Females sport horns of a similar length but more slender. Horns, which are not shed, grow continually and develop annual growth rings that reflect a goat's age.

Black hooves have cushioned skid-proof pads for grip and traction on steep, rocky surfaces.

Mountain goats reach 60 to 70 inches long, 35 to 45 inches high and weigh 150 to 300 pounds.

(William Wakeland)

Mountain goats may be confused with Dall sheep, but the shaggy coat, deep chest, beard and black horns distinguish goats from sheep. From a distance, goats appear pure white, sheep look slightly yellowish.

Range: Mountain goats inhabit mountains throughout Southeast, and north and west along the coastal mountains to Cook Inlet. In Southcentral, goats are generally limited to the Chugach and Wrangell mountains, although their

(George Wuerthner)

range extends into the
Talkeetna Mountains nearly
to Denali National Park.

Goats were transplanted to Kodiak Island, and to Baranof
and Revillagigedo islands where they are now well-
established.

Food: Mountain goats both graze and browse, depending
on habitat and season. In summer they graze on grasses,
herbs and low shrubs in alpine meadows. As winter cold
kills succulents, they shift to browsing. Hemlock provides
important winter nutrition, but the goats eat whatever plant
material is available.

Life History: Breeding occurs in November and December,
and billies wander some distance searching for females.
Males do not collect harems, but they do fight, sometimes
leaving punctures on the rear quarters of their opponents.

Except during the rut, adult males usually remain apart from other goats. Females with kids and immature goats generally form groups.

A single kid 12 inches long, weighing 6 or 7 pounds, is born in late May or early June after a gestation period of about 180 days. In rare cases twins are born. Kids can keep up with adults when only hours old. Nannies seek solitude prior to giving birth, but shortly join other nannies with newborns to form nursery herds. Kids usually remain with their mothers until the following breeding season, but goats may not breed every year.

Mountain goats may live 14 to 15 years. Productivity of most mountain goat herds is low, and several years must pass for a herd to recover from losses due to overhunting, predation or starvation during a severe winter. ▪

Arctic Hare
Lepus othus

Description: In summer, arctic hares sport a dusky brown coat, finely grizzled with gray, that is more gray on the sides and darkening on the top of the head. Their underparts are white. Dark cinnamon or buffy hair marks their nose and mouth. A white ring circles each dark-colored eye. Their ears are dusky, washing with gray and tipped with black. In winter, they become all white with black-tipped ears.

Arctic hares may reach 28 inches in length and weigh up to 12 pounds.

Range: Arctic hares range the Alaska Peninsula, and the west coast of Alaska from Bristol Bay north to around Kotzebue. Populations are low and declining throughout much of their range.

Food: Their diet consists of willow — the leaves, bark, twigs, buds and roots — and grasses, flowers, stems and leaves of saxifrage, and buds and twigs of crowberry.

Arctic hares living near the coast will eat kelp at low tide as well as other marine plants. They also eat carrion.

Life History: Arctic hares produce a litter of six or seven annually, usually about the time

(Leroy Anderson)

the snow disappears. They prefer open upland tundra and windswept rocky slopes where they can use the claws of their middle toes to dig through the snow for food, which they locate by smell.

Scientists at the Institute of Arctic Biology, University of Alaska Fairbanks, estimate that arctic hares may reach a maximum life expectancy of about 10 years, with an average of about 3 years in the wild. They base their estimates, in part, on the larger body size of the arctic hare compared to the snowshoe hare. ■

Snowshoe Hare

Lepus americanus

(George Wuerthner)

Description: In summer, snowshoe hare are grayish to brown, with a slightly darker rump and midline on their back. Their tail is dark above, lighter beneath; their abdomen and chin are white, their throat buffy to reddish-brown.

In winter, snowshoe hare appear pure white with dark-tipped ears. Their dark eyes, nose and ear tips are sometimes the only parts of the animal visible in the snow.

This species has big feet covered with coarse hair and long toes that can be spread wide to enable it to travel easily over the deepest snow.

Snowshoe hare grow to 18 or 20 inches and weigh 3 to 4 pounds.

Range: This species is the common snowshoe hare or varying hare of the northern half of North America. In Alaska, it occurs in suitable habitat throughout the state except for the lower portion of the Alaska Peninsula, the northern part of the arctic coast and most islands. It is relatively scarce in Southeast.

Food: Snowshoe hare feed on grasses, buds, twigs and leaves during summer. In winter, they eat twigs and needles of spruce and the bark and buds of many plants including willow, cottonwood, birch, aspen, alder and hemlock.

Life History: Snowshoe hare reach sexual maturity at about age 1. They produce a litter averaging four young, called leverets, in mid-May after a 36-day gestation period. Females breed immediately after giving birth, thus typically producing more than one litter each year.

The female bears her young in an unlined depression, called a form. Newborns weigh 2 ounces and can walk by the time their fur is dry. Within a couple of days they move about the form, and by 12 to 14 days they are eating green vegetation. The general public sometimes refers to snowshoe hare as rabbits, but newborn hare are fully furred with their eyes wide open, whereas newborn rabbits are blind and hairless.

Snowshoe hare populations fluctuate dramatically, with highs and lows occurring roughly 10 years apart. All areas do not experience highs and lows at the same time. The cycles seem to progress from east to west and to be less pronounced near the coasts.

Snowshoe hares have been known to live 8 years in captivity, with an average of about 5 to 7 years. They live an average of 1 1/2 to 2 years in the wild. ■

Brown Lemming
Lemmus sibiricus

Description: Brown lemmings maintain their tawny or reddish-colored coat year-round, although in summer their color may shift to grayish. These thickset rodents have long, loose fur; small ears; and a short, hairy tail. Well-developed claws protrude from large, strong forefeet.

Individuals weigh from 2 1/2 to 4 ounces and reach 5 to 5 1/2 inches in length; their tail adds another two-thirds of an inch to their total length. Sexes are identical in size and color.

Range: The most widespread of Alaska's true lemmings, this species ranges throughout northern Alaska and the Alaska Peninsula in open tundra; it does not occur in Southeast, Southcentral or on the Kodiak island group.

(Jim Helmericks)

Food: Brown lemmings feed primarily on grasses, sedges, seeds, willow bark and probably insects. Evidence indicates lemmings are cannibalistic when food is scarce.

Life History: This species may breed all winter, but is more likely to breed from June to September. Females can become pregnant at two weeks, and give birth to an average of 7 young per litter. Newborns weigh about 1/10 of an ounce, but develop rapidly, opening their eyes at 11 days and walking at 15 days.

Lemmings remain active year-round, selecting low-lying areas with maximum snow cover for their winter nests. They wear tiny trails beneath the snow going to and from their nests.

Lemming populations fluctuate dramatically, giving this family a reputation for suicidal migrations that is more fiction than fact. Why their numbers change so drastically is not clear, but is likely related to predation, food supply, weather and perhaps genetic changes in individuals within a population. Lemmings do not migrate; in times of stress, animals may move to the edges of their home area and this might explain their presence on sea ice and in other inappropriate habitat.

Their life expectancy is 1 to 2 years. ■

Collared Lemming
Dicrostonyx torquatus

Description: A species related to but not actually a true
lemming is the collared lemming, unique among rodents
because it changes color to adapt to winter's white
environment. In summer, collared lemmings are grayish to
buffy with an irregular black line extending from their
forehead to their tail and a tawny collar reaching to their
armpits.

In winter, their long, soft fur becomes pure white. Also, the
third and fourth claws on their forefeet enlarge to aid in
digging through snow. These claws are worn to the size of the
other claws by spring.

Collared lemmings grow to about 5 inches and have a
short tail about 1/3 of an inch. They weigh about an ounce.

Range: This species occurs in Alaska, northern Canada,
along a strip of Greenland and across Eurasia. In Alaska
they are found from the Brooks Range north, in coastal
Alaska from the Kuskokwim River drainage north. They also
inhabit Unalaska and Umnak islands in the Aleutians and
St. Lawrence Island in the Bering Sea. There are several
subspecies of collared lemming including St. Lawrence Island
(*D.t. exsul*), Bering (*D.t. rubricatus*), Nelson's (*D.t. nelsoni*)
and Unalaska (*D.t. unalascensis*).

Food: Like true lemmings, collared lemmings eat mostly
plants including sedges, bearberry, cottongrass and saxifrage.
They may eat insects and meat when available.

Life History: Collared lemmings live in burrows from 2 to
3 feet long, with a grass- and moss-lined nest chamber
several inches long at one end. A satellite burrow near the
nest chamber serves as a sanitary area. They prefer dry,

(Chlaus Lotscher)

sandy or gravelly habitat above
tree line where they can use
their strong winter claws to dig through wind-blown snow.

Breeding usually occurs from March to September,
although it can take place earlier. Females can bear three
litters annually with an average of 4 1/2 young per litter.
Individuals seldom live more than a year or two in the wild.
With its rapid breeding pace and short life span, it is not
unusual for an entire population to turn over in a season. ■

Northern Bog Lemming
Synaptomys borealis

Description: A coat grizzled brown above and dirty whitish below marks this species of bog lemming, sometimes called a lemming mouse. This species, not a true lemming but a related species, resembles the short-tailed *Microtus* vole because it has a thickset body, a short tail and coarse fur. Its upper incisors have a longitudinal groove; true lemmings have ungrooved teeth.

The smallest of the lemmings in Alaska, individuals reach 4 to 5 inches and weigh a little more than an ounce.

Range: Northern bog lemmings occur in meadows and bogs from the Bering Sea coast south through Southcentral and Southeast and continuing south to northern Washington state. A smaller, related species is found in the northeastern United States.

Food: They feed on low vegetation such as bulbs, grasses, succulent herbs and probably slugs, snails and insects.

Life History: This species breeds mostly in the summer, although it can breed earlier in the year. Females usually produce three litters annually.

Northern bog lemmings occupy warmer climates than Alaska's other lemming species and their fur is not as thick. They build runways and excavate tunnels through their territory, and sometimes rely on the pathways of other small mammals.

They are known to have lived 2 1/2 years. ■

Mountain Lion or Cougar or Puma
Felis concolor

Description: Color of coat varies from rufous to tawny, buff or gray, with a buff-colored belly and white chest and throat. Northern animals have long, soft hair. Mountain lions have a small head in proportion to body size; hind legs longer than front legs; five toes on the front paws, four on the back; and a tail nearly one-third of their total length.

They are the largest cat native to North America excluding the jaguar. Males average 5 1/2 to 8 feet in length and weigh 125 pounds on average; females are smaller. Large males have been measured at 9 feet with a weight of 225 pounds.

Range: Mountain lions ranged historically from Alaska south throughout North America and south again as far as Patagonia in southern South America. They are now primarily confined to pockets in the western United States and Canada, with a remnant population in Florida and perhaps in the Appalachian Mountains. There may still be a few individuals in Central and South America. In 1989, a mountain lion was killed near Wrangell in Southeast. Although rare, reports of mountain lion sightings in Southeast and eastcentral Alaska are increasing. University of Alaska Museum scientists speculate this increase may be due to an expansion of mule deer into eastcentral Alaska.

Food: They chiefly eat deer and elk, but will eat moose, mountain goat, coyote, snowshoe hare, porcupine or raccoon. They will normally drag their prey some distance from the kill site, eat a portion and bury the remainder under leaves or brush for later consumption.

Life History: Mountain lions, like all cats, are polygamous. Breeding usually occurs late in the year during the nine-day period when females are in heat. One to five, usually three or four, kittens are born 90 to 96 days later in rock crevices or other sheltered spots. Kittens can be born any time of the year, but are usually born in late winter or early spring. Newborns are 10 inches long and weigh about 12 ounces. Kittens born in winter and spring can hunt with their mother in late fall and kill their own prey by winter's end. They usually remain with their family for several more months. Females normally breed every two years.

Secretive mountain lions routinely patrol an area of from five to 25 square miles, which they mark by scraping together mounds of brush soaked with urine and sometimes mixed with scat. A mountain lion does not specifically defend its home range, but marking the area seems to discourage intrusion by others.

They are usually silent; they do not roar, but females can scream and both sexes can produce a variety of sounds.

Mountain lions typically live 10 to 15 years in the wild; captives have lived 18 years. ■

(Tom Soucek)

Lynx
Felis lynx

Description: Lynx are gray, streaked with black on their neck ruff, forehead, back and legs. Their short tail has black encircling its tip. Lynx have a chunky appearance, with long, usually tufted ears, long legs and exceptionally large feet that enable them to move easily in deep snow.

Lynx grow to 30 or 40 inches in length, stand 24 to

(Tom Soucek)

28 inches high at the shoulders, and weigh 13 to 30 pounds, with some males weighing even more.

Range: Lynx are found throughout mainland Alaska except on the Yukon-Kuskokwim delta and on the southern flank of the Alaska Peninsula. They are scarce along the northern Gulf of Alaska coast and in Southeast, where they occur mainly in large river valleys. Their favored habitat is mature forests with dense undercover.

Food: With their own survival tightly interwoven with that of their main prey, snowshoe hare, lynx populations follow those of the hare. When snowshoe hare increase, so do lynx. Since the hare have a roughly 10-year cycle of abundance, so do lynx. When hare numbers decline, lynx quickly starve out, and remain scarce until hare populations rebound. Being predators, lynx will take other prey on occasion such as small deer, grouse, mice, even caribou, Dall sheep and fox. They are not fond of fish, although they have been found to feed on salmon.

Life History: Breeding occurs in March or April, with a gestation period of 60 days. Usually two to four kittens are born in a natural den: a hollow tree or log, under a rock cliff or under a dense pile of brush. When lynx populations are increasing, females breed in their first year and large litters and high survival rates among kittens are common. When snowshoe hare populations decline, female lynx may not breed their first year, fewer kittens are born and their survival rate is lower.

Lynx are adept climbers and swimmers. Although they usually remain in the same general area, they will move to new territory if forced out by lack of prey.

Individuals have been known to live more than 25 years in captivity. ■

Arctic or Brooks Range Marmot
Marmota broweri

Left to right, woodchuck (groundhog), hoary marmot, arctic marmot. Animals are anesthetized. (Dr. Tom Albert)

Description: Closely related to the hoary marmot, the arctic marmot's coat is gray with dark-tipped hairs. Its face and rump are darker than that of the hoary marmot, and it lacks the light patch on the snout of the hoary marmot. Its tail is reddish with a black tip. The arctic marmot has a stubby body; short, broad head; short legs; small ears and densely furred tail. Its fur is much softer than that of the hoary marmot. Arctic marmots emit an ear-piercing, shrill call when alarmed.

The arctic marmot grows to more than 2 feet and weighs 10 pounds or more.

Range: This species inhabits talus slopes throughout much of the Brooks Range.

Food: The arctic marmot eats grasses, flowering plants, berries, roots, mosses and lichens.

Life History: This species reaches sexual maturity at age 2 or 3. It breeds in April or May, while still in its winter den, and about 30 days later the female bears two to six young. When the young are about 2 months old, they strike out on their own.

(Dr. Tom Albert)

Marmots are colonial, and while each family maintains its own burrow, they settle close to their neighbors in the same talus slope. Rocks in the talus slope provide perches from which to spot predators, including golden eagles. Their summer houses have several entrances leading to a grass-lined den. Because of their northerly habitat, arctic marmots build special winter dens with one entrance on a windswept ridge that becomes snow-free in early spring. When all members of the colony are inside the den, usually by September, they plug the entrance with dirt, vegetation and feces, and then hibernate. No animals can leave the den until the plug melts the following May.

Scientists differ on the common name for this species. Some maintain that since this species has a smaller range than that of the state's other marmot species, its common name should reflect that common range, i.e. arctic marmot or Brooks Range marmot. Other scientists say that Alaska marmot is the appropriate common name because the state's other species of marmots have a range that extends well beyond Alaska's boundaries.

Arctic marmots live to about age 5 in the wild. ■

Hoary Marmot
Marmota caligata

(Patrick J. Endres)

Description: A relative of the squirrel, these large burrowing mammals sport grizzled gray upperparts, from which they earn their name "hoary," and a buff rump and lower back. The black on their face shades to a whitish area in front of their eyes. Their underside is light-colored; their tail is buff tipped with brown on the top, dark brown below. Their feet are blackish, from whence comes their species name, *caligata*, meaning "boots." They have stiff fur, unlike the Alaska marmot that has soft fur.

Males reach 30 inches, females slightly less; they typically weigh 10 pounds or more.

Range: Hoary marmots occur throughout mountainous regions of the Interior, Southcentral and Southwest.

Food: They eat primarily grasses, flowering plants, berries, roots, mosses and lichens.

Life History: Hoary marmots breed when they come out of hibernation in April and May. In the only litter of the year, two to six young are born about a month after mating. Young remain with their family group until they are about 2 months old, when they move out on their own.

Hoary marmots excavate burrows and dens at the base of talus slopes, where the rocks provide safety and lookout posts to spot predators. They live in colonies but each family has its own burrow and den. Unlike the arctic marmot, the hoary marmot lives year-round in the same burrow-den complex, plugging the tunnel to its den with dirt, vegetation and feces when it is time to hibernate in the fall.

Marmots communicate with one another with a variety of sounds, one of which, a distinct whistle, frequently confounds hikers in the high country.

Hoary marmots live to about age 5 in the wild. ■

Marten
Martes americana

Description: Marten vary in color from pale yellow to dark chocolate brown, deepening to black on the feet and end of tail. A broad streak of lighter fur runs from the throat down the front of the neck onto the chest and reaches irregularly to the insides of the forelegs.

Marten have a sharp, foxlike face, black nose pad and whiskers. Their ears are broad and rounded, and unlike other members of the weasel family, they have a long bushy tail. Their large, furred feet aid their movement on snow and their powerful, non-retractable claws enable them to climb trees easily and to hold their prey. Marten have a well-defined scent gland about 3 inches long and 1 inch wide on the center of their abdomen.

Marten fur is long, durable and beautiful. Frequently called American sable, marten are slightly smaller than European sable, with similar fur.

Males grow to 10 to 25 inches long, plus an 8-inch tail, and weigh 3 pounds; females are substantially smaller.

(Ernest Manewal)

Range: Marten need mature conifer forests to survive, and their range in Alaska coincides with these mature stands. They are found throughout timbered Alaska, except north of the Brooks Range and on the Yukon-Kuskokwim delta. They do not inhabit Kodiak Island or the islands of Prince William Sound.

(Tom Soucek)

Food: Marten usually forage
at night and rely primarily
on microtine rodents for food, but they also eat snowshoe
hare, bird eggs and chicks, insects, carrion and berries and
other vegetation.

Life History: Attaining sexual maturity in two years,
marten breed during the summer. Two to four young are
born in April, after a gestation period of 220 to 290 days,
of which about five months is due to delayed implantation.
Their den is in a hollow tree or log where the 6-inch-long
young are born blind and helpless. They develop slowly and
grow to about half of adult size by mid-July. The female
raises the young by herself; by fall they are independent,
and leave their mother to become solitary hunters.

Females have been known to live at least until age 12 in
the wild; captive marten have reached age 17. ■

House Mouse
Mus musculus

(Leonard Lee Rue III)

Description: Brownish-gray above and lighter underneath, the house mouse has a slender body, large ears and small feet. It grows to 7 inches, including a 3 1/2-inch, sparsely haired tail.

Range: In Alaska, house mice occur mainly in seaports, although they have found their way into most larger human communities, except perhaps far northern rural villages.

Food: Although they are omnivorous, house mice prefer grain and vegetables.

Life History: Females breed at 6 weeks to 2 months of age, and after a gestation of 19 to 31 days produce a litter of from four to nine blind, naked and helpless young. Several litters may be born each year.

Young are soon able to follow their mother on foraging expeditions, and they usually scatter and fend for themselves when about half grown, or at 3 to 4 weeks.

House mice do not hibernate, and have only a slight storage instinct.

Their life span is about 5 years. ∎

Keen's Deer Mouse

Peromyscus keeni

Description: Deer mice are covered with soft hair, dark brown above and white below. Their name comes from the resemblance of their coat's pattern and color to that of white-tailed deer. In contrast to the naked tail of house mice, deer mice have a well-haired tail with scaly **annulations**. They have fairly large ears, only thinly covered by hair, and large eyes.

(Leonard Lee Rue III)

Deer mice emit several sounds including squeaks and buzzes, and when excited, they have been reported to beat their front feet rapidly, somewhat like beating a drum.

Their long tail makes up about half the 7- to 8-inch length of these medium-sized mice.

Range: Deer mice occur where there is suitable habitat — timber and brush — in Southeast. Several subspecies have been listed; they differ slightly in size, skull characteristics and color. Keen's deer mouse occurs throughout Southeast from Glacier Bay east to Haines and Skagway and southward.

Deer mice are a far-ranging clan found widely over North America from near the Arctic Circle to deserts of the Lower 48, and from near sea level to near tree line. *P. maniculatus* is the most widely distributed of the many species of deer mice.

Food: Deer mice are omnivorous, but their main food seems to be dried seeds and, where available, nuts and berries. They also eat insects, worms, bird eggs, young birds, dead mice and carrion of almost any type.

Life History: In Alaska, this species probably produces only one brood, averaging four, a year. Usually the young are capable of living on their own about a month after birth.

Deer mice, which keep their bodies immaculate, build cup-shaped nests in abandoned burrows or in hollow logs, stumps, tree root cavities or any sheltered spot. This largely nocturnal species is commonly found living in old cabins. They store seeds and other foods in winter, and though they do not hibernate, they may spend many hours curled up in their warm nests during the coldest days.

Scientists estimate deer mice in the wild live less than 2 years; captive animals have reached more than 8 years. ■

Meadow Jumping Mouse
Zapus hudsonius

Description: The tricolored coat of *Zapus* is dark above, yellow on the sides and white underneath. In winter, the colors blend and become less distinct.

These medium-sized mice have short forelegs, but greatly lengthened hind legs, and a long, slender, tapering tail that takes up about 5 inches of their 8 1/2-inch total length.

The other species of *Zapus* found in Alaska, *Z. princeps*, or western jumping mouse, is about 10 inches long, has a tail of 5 1/2 inches and hind feet more than an inch long.

Range: Meadow jumping mice range throughout the southern half of Alaska, including the Alaska Peninsula, Kenai Peninsula and from the Alaska Range to the Gulf of Alaska. They have also been found in Fairbanks, Haines, Skagway and on Revillagigedo Island where Ketchikan is located. Their territory extends in a band across North America, encompassing much of southern Canada and the northeastern third of the United States and extending south to Georgia. Isolated populations live in the mountains of Arizona and New Mexico.

Meadow jumping mouse. (Leonard Lee Rue III)

Western jumping mice occur along the coast of Southeast from the Taku River drainage south.

Jumping mice are erratic in distribution, more often rare than common and yet in some areas fairly abundant.

Food: Jumping mice feed on vegetation, seeds and nuts, grains, fungus, berries, fruits and insects.

Life History: Meadow jumping mice may produce up to three litters annually, each averaging five young; in Alaska it is likely they produce fewer litters.

Summer nests are made in shallow burrows or on the ground. Hibernating nests may be dug 3 feet or more into the ground where individuals or groups spend the winter. *Zapus* usually spend more than half of their lives hibernating. Their body temperature can drop as much as 35 degrees F when they are hibernating.

Zapus are found in forests, and on moist plains where they prefer brush and shrub-lined streams. Jumping mice are fond of meadows and grassy areas, and in daytime may be flushed into jumping across the turf. Although they are reported to be capable of jumping more than 3 feet in a single bound, jumping mice normally move slowly on all four feet. They are also adept climbers and swimmers.

Zapus princeps is known to live 4 years in the wild; *Zapus hudsonius* has lived 5 years in captivity. ■

Mink

Mustela vison

Description: Mink are rich dark brown, or russet brown, with a white chin and irregular white spots on the throat and breast. They have a long body and neck that contrasts with their short head and pointed muzzle. Their legs are short, and their tail long and bushy.

Mink weigh from 2 to 4, and occasionally 5, pounds; grow from 20 to 33 inches long and stand 5 to 6 inches at the shoulder. Females are about half the size of males.

Mink are just one of several members of the Mustelid family found in Alaska. They are considerably larger than weasels, almost always darker than weasels in summer, and

(Tom Soucek)

lack the extensive white found on the underside of weasels. Marten are yellower with an orangish chest patch, and a more bushy tail.

Range: Mink are common throughout Alaska except in the Kodiak archipelago, Aleutian Islands, offshore islands of the Bering Sea and most of the Arctic Slope.

Food: Mink eat what they can catch. Fish, snowshoe hare, rodents, birds and insects are taken wherever available. They hunt well on land and in the water. They catch fish while swimming — mink can travel 40 to 50 feet or more underwater — and will attack wild ducks. In coastal areas they eat carrion or catch fish and crustaceans trapped in tidal pools.

Life History: Mink have musk glands and deposit the musk around their territory as the breeding season approaches. Breeding takes place from March through late April. A litter that averages five is born 40 to 75 days later, with the variability due to delayed implantation. Most newborns, 4 or 5 inches long and covered with fine, short, whitish hairs, arrive in mid-June. Their eyes open at 5 weeks, at which time the young are weaned and live entirely on meat. Families break up later in the summer; thereafter mink are solitary until the breeding season.

Mink live about 10 years in the wild. ■

Moose
Alces alces

(Tim Van Nest)

Description: Moose are colored a variety of browns, shading from pale yellow to black, depending on the age of the animal and the season. They have a tiny tail, long legs, a short body, a great drooping nose and a bell — a simple skin tab hanging from the lower neck that sometimes measures 2 or more feet — that has no known function.

Alaska moose are the largest of their species, which is the largest living member of the deer family. They have a length of 8 to 10 feet and stand 4 1/2 to 8 feet at the shoulder. Males usually weigh 1,000 to 1,600 pounds, although larger individuals have been recorded. Cows reach 800 to 1,200 pounds.

Only bulls grow antlers. Males carry the largest antlers when they are age 6 to 12. The largest moose antlers in North America come from Alaska, where racks measuring 6 feet from tip to tip are seen occasionally.

Range: Moose occur in suitable habitat from the Unuk River in Southeast to the North Slope. They are not found on most major islands of Southeast, on islands of Prince William Sound, on the Kodiak group or on any offshore islands of the Bering Sea. Moose range south on the Alaska Peninsula to Cold Bay. In the 1970s, moose in numbers moved onto the Seward Peninsula for the first time in recorded history.

Food: Fall and winter find moose browsing on willow, birch and aspen twigs. In spring they graze grasses, sedges, pond weeds and other new shoots. In some areas, moose feed on plants in shallow ponds all summer and into fall; in other areas, birch, willow and aspen sustain them in summer.

Life History: Moose breed in the fall, in late September and early October. Cows generally are ready for breeding between ages 16 and 28 months. They carry the fetus about eight months before giving birth in late May and early June. Older cows, on good range, have twins from 15 to 60 percent of the time, depending on the condition of the cow and quality of the range. Triplets occur occasionally.

Most calves, reddish-brown at birth and weighing 25 to 35 pounds, are born in swampy muskegs. Young are weaned by fall, but remain with their mother through the winter, even though calves often survive on their own if necessary.

In spring, newborns may represent 40 to 50 percent of a moose population, but mortality may be high, and by November their numbers may be reduced by half. Severe weather and predation may cause high mortality.

Moose do not migrate in the classic sense, but periodic movements of considerable distance and/or elevation are made with changes in the season. The same animals repeat these movements year after year, and construction of pipelines, highways, fences and other structures can impact moose movements adversely.

Records indicate that moose can live to 27 years. ◼

Muskoxen
Ovibos moschatus

Description: Muskoxen are hump-shouldered, shaggy, sway-backed, hoofed mammals whose size is exaggerated by a heavy coat of extremely long, coarse, outer hair that is dark brown except for a light tan saddle and legs. During spring and summer muskoxen acquire an even shaggier appearance when they shed their fine, light brown under-hair in great trailing strands. Their underhair, known as *qiviut*, is so dense that it protects the animal from cold and frost.

The amber-to-black horns of muskoxen descend and rise to the sides in a graceful sweep. Bulls have longer, heavier horns than cows. Muskoxen are 6 to 7 or more feet long. Adult bulls stand 5 feet at the shoulder, females are a foot shorter. Adult bulls weigh up to about 800 pounds; cows weigh 500 to 600 pounds.

(Patrick J. Endres)

Range: Muskoxen occur on Nunivak Island, Nelson Island, the Seward Peninsula, Cape Thompson and the North Slope. These herds descend from 34 Greenland muskoxen brought to the University of Alaska Fairbanks in the early 1930s after hunters killed the last muskoxen in Alaska in 1865. In 1935-36, the surviving muskoxen were moved from Fairbanks to Nunivak Island. By 1968 they numbered 750 animals. From this nucleus, muskoxen were transplanted to other areas in Alaska, with the goal of restoring the species to its original Alaska range.

Food: In summer, muskoxen prefer moist habitat. On Nunivak they eat sedges, cottongrass, horsetails, bluejoint and fescue grass, cloudberry, nagoonberry, diamond-leaf willow and dwarf birch. During winters on Nunivak, they eat beach rye grass, sedges, wood rushes, fescue grass, crowberry and dwarf birch and willow.

   Captive animals eat grains and hay, much like domestic livestock.

Life History: Nunivak Island muskoxen breed during late July and August. Bulls probably mature at ages 4 to 6, but older, dominant bulls keep younger ones from breeding. Young and very old bulls that have been pushed out of a herd may wander on their own or band together in smaller groups and rejoin the main herds for winter. Cows may mature at age 2 and bear a calf at age 3, provided they have good nutrition. When well fed, cows can produce a calf each year, but on poor range a cow may give birth only every other year. Calves are born in late April and early May on Nunivak; they weigh 25 to 35 pounds at birth, and reach 100 to 170 pounds their first year.

   Records indicate muskoxen have lived to age 24 in the wild. ■

Muskrat

Ondatra zibethicus

(Jon R. Nickles)

Description: Muskrats are dark brown to silvery brown with lighter underparts. Young appear duller and lighter-colored.

Muskrats have a robust, compact body; short legs; and strong hind feet partially webbed and modified for swimming. Their long, scaly and nearly naked tail is strongly flattened vertically to serve as a rudder and a scull in the water.

Nearly as fine and dense as beaver fur, muskrat fur shields these animals from the cold water in which they spend much of their lives. Their coat consists of short, dense underfur, and longer, glistening guard hairs. They can be distinguished from beavers by their ratlike tail and smaller size.

Muskrat size varies with their location. For example, upper Yukon River muskrats are larger than those found downriver. Most animals measure 18 to 25 inches, and weigh 2 to 4 pounds.

Range: Muskrats occur throughout all of mainland Alaska south of the Brooks Range except for the Alaska Peninsula west of the Ugashik lakes. They were introduced to large islands of the Kodiak group but are absent from most other Alaska islands.

Food: Muskrats eat sedges, grasses, a variety of aquatic plants such as the roots and stems of cattails, bulrushes and lilies, invertebrates, and occasionally mussels, shrimp and small fish.

Life History: Females, which reach sexual maturity at 9 to 10 months, usually produce two litters during the breeding season that begins in spring when open water is available. In the Interior, the first breeding occurs from late April to mid-May with seven to eight young born about 25 days later. A few days after the first litter is born, females breed again.

Never found far from water, muskrats occur in greatest numbers around marshes, lakes, ponds and rivers. Their densest populations are found in the Yukon Flats, Minto Flats, at Tetlin Lakes, on the Yukon-Kuskokwim delta and in the Selawik-Kobuk-Noatak area of northwestern Alaska. The telltale sign of their presence is the houses, or pushups, they build of rushes and water plants. Sometimes 2 to 3 feet above the water's surface and 5 to 6 feet in diameter, pushups are built primarily as winter feeding and resting areas. They are insulated by snow, and a visiting muskrat can breathe through the snow covering while it feeds.

Winter takes its toll on muskrats when the ice becomes too thick and limits feeding areas, or when high water in spring floods their houses, making them vulnerable to predators or hunters and trappers.

Muskrats live about 3 years in the wild, up to 10 years in captivity.

River Otter
Lontra canadensis

Description: Dense brown fur shading to a lighter color on the underparts, chin and throat characterizes this species' coat.

River otters have a powerful, low-slung, long, slender body, long neck and flattened head. Their tail is long and tapered, their legs short, their feet webbed. As with most members of the Mustelid or weasel family, they have anal glands that can produce an unpleasant odor. Large males grow from 3 1/2 to almost 5 feet long, and stand 9 to 10 inches at shoulder height. River otters weigh 15 to 35 pounds; females are about a quarter smaller than males.

(Harry M. Walker)

Range: This species is found throughout the state except on the Aleutian Islands, Bering Sea islands and on the arctic coastal plain east of Point Lay.

Food: Chiefly fish eaters, river otters will consume a variety of available food including shellfish, insects, frogs, birds, eggs, small mammals and vegetation. They kill and eat muskrats at times; at other times the two species seem to live together peacefully.

Life History: Breeding usually occurs in May. After delayed implantation, one to six young, typically two or three, are born nine to 13 months later in a riverbank den. Dark-colored, blind newborns are about the size of a small ground squirrel. Their eyes open after about 1 month. They learn to swim at about 2 months but continue to nurse for another month or two. They remain with their mother for about the first year of their life.

River otters are agile, playful movers. They can swim 6 mph or spurt even faster by porpoising on the surface. They can dive to at least 60 feet, run as fast as a human and speed to 15 mph by running and sliding on hard snow and ice. They appear to enjoy play, using rocks and sticks as props for their antics.

River otters can reproduce in the wild at least until age 20 and are known to reach age 23 in captivity. ■

Sea Otter
Enhydra lutris

(Lon E. Lauber)

Description: The sea otter has the densest fur of any mammal. Its coat consists of sparse guard hairs and an underfur of inch-long fibers so compact that the underfur averages 300,000 hairs per square inch. Sea otters appear brown but their underfur ranges from brown, sometimes with reddish tinges, to nearly black; guard hairs may be black, pale brown or silvery. Older animals develop a whitish-silvery head.

Sea otters have a broad head and small ears. Their tail is long and flat. They propel themselves through the water with large, webbed hind feet. The short toes on their front feet are used to manipulate food. Sea otters do not have the anal scent glands characteristic of most members of the weasel family, to which they belong.

Adult males, largest member of the Mustelid family, reach 5 feet and average 80 pounds; some individuals top the scale at 100 pounds. Females average 4 feet and 60 pounds.

Range: Sea otters originally inhabited coastal waters from Baja California to the northern Japanese home islands. In Alaska, they occurred in coastal waters in a huge arc from Southeast to the extreme western Aleutians. Commercial hunting nearly wiped out the species, but several small groups survived. The Alaska population has expanded from these remnant groups and from groups reintroduced to sites in Southeast.

Sea otters were also transplanted to the coasts of British Columbia, Washington and Oregon.

Food: Sea otters eat primarily clams, mussels, snails, abalone, sea urchins, crabs, octopus and, in areas where invertebrate populations have been reduced, slow-moving bottomfish. They may eat up to 25 pounds of fresh food daily, among the highest known food requirement for any animal of this size.

Although they are a marine mammal, sea otters usually confine their foraging to nearshore waters. In the Aleutians, they typically dive to more than 130 feet on feeding forays, deeper than in some other parts of their range. Sea otters have been recorded diving to more than 320 feet.

One of the few mammal species known to use tools, sea otters feed while floating on their back. They put a rock on their chest and break the shells of shellfish and mollusks against the rock to reach the softer flesh inside.

Life History: Adults reach sexual maturity at ages 4 to 6. Breeding and pupping occur year-round. Each female normally produces one pup every one to two years. Pup survival rates are high when food is abundant, allowing sea otter populations to increase rapidly.

Air trapped in their dense fur buoys sea otters and helps keep them warm. They lack the layer of blubber found on other marine mammals, so their fur must be kept absolutely clean to prevent water from touching their skin. Sea otters spend much time grooming their fur, ensuring that the trapped air remains and that the animal stays warm. Soiled fur allows water to penetrate, causing the animal to chill and die. Oil spills present special hazards to sea otters.

Many otters live to about age 20, perhaps a bit more. ■

Collared Pika
Ochotona collaris

Description: Pikas have a grayish or buffy coat that
lightens on the underside, and brownish or blackish ears.
A band of light gray circles their neck and joins with the
lighter undersides.

Pikas have soft, dense fur; broad, rounded ears; a
chunky body and short legs. Their rear legs are only slightly
longer than the front, and they run rather than hop. The
soles of their feet are fur-clad, which enhances insulation
against the cold. Sharp, curved claws aid climbing on
steep surfaces. They have no visible tail and their eyes are
placed so they can see to the front as well as to the sides.

Pikas reach 6 to 8 inches and weigh from 4 to 8 ounces.

Range: Collared pikas — northern representatives of a
genus that is distributed throughout the Rocky Mountains
and the Cascade ranges of
Oregon, Washington and

(William Wakeland)

California — are found in central and southern Alaska and in Yukon Territory.

Food: Pikas eat all species of edible plants they find growing near their rocky homes. They also cut and dry the same plants to store for winter use. Tiny haystacks stashed throughout a rocky slope indicate pikas have been busy in the area. The actual variety of plants eaten depends on location and an individual pika's preference. Their selections range from spruce, berries and various flowering plants to grasses.

Life History: Young, which weigh about 1/3 ounce at birth, may be born in any month from May to September following a 30-day gestation period. Litters have from two to six youngsters that grow quickly and are weaned when only one-fourth to one-third grown. Females may breed again, producing two litters in one season.

Pikas are vulnerable to predators such as weasels and birds of prey. They rely on eyesight, hearing, camouflage, stealth, quick movements, a well-stocked winter food supply of hay and the inaccessibility of their rock-slide home for survival. They normally live in colonies, but each animal has its own turf so the colony is dispersed across a rocky slope. They lessen their defense of territorial boundaries during the breeding season, but vigorously defend their stashed food supplies as winter approaches. Pikas do not hibernate, and their survival through the winter requires an abundant food supply.

Pikas live about 3 years. ■

Porcupine
Erethizon dorsatum

(Chlaus Lotscher)

Description: Despite their distinct yellowish cast, Alaska porcupines are basically slaty black or brown with lighter-tipped hairs. Incisor teeth are orange.

They have a thick, heavy body, a proportionally small head, short legs, and a short, thick tail. These rodents are covered with long, soft, woolly hair that is interspersed with hard, glistening hairs and stiff, sharp, hollow spines, many of which have barbs.

Adult porcupines reach 31 to 33 inches including a 6-inch tail. Adult males weigh from 15 to 18 pounds with some males reaching 25 pounds. Females average a couple of pounds smaller.

Range: Porcupines occur throughout most of Alaska except on Kodiak, Nunivak and St. Lawrence islands. They prefer forests but have been spotted living among the willows and alders that trail across treeless portions of the Alaska Peninsula.

Food: In summer, porcupines eat a variety of vegetation including leaves, buds and twigs of shrubs, trees and forbs. Their vegetarian diet lacks the sodium necessary for their body to properly balance its potassium levels, so porcupines visit natural salt licks, or get their needed sodium from human perspiration on tools, plywood glue, road salt, some paints, shed antlers and bones of carcasses. In winter, they concentrate on the cambium or inner bark of spruce, birch and aspen.

Life History: Breeding generally occurs in November, following which a single young is born in about 16 weeks. Its soft, moist quills dry and stiffen quickly, enabling the youngster to protect itself shortly after birth.

Solitary porcupines are primarily nocturnal, although they can be spotted slowly crossing a road or moving through the forest early and late in the day. In winter, hikers may spot them well up in a conifer, chewing on the bark. Despite common folklore, porcupines do not throw their quills. Instead, when threatened, they raise their quills, turn their back and switch their tail vigorously, a behavior that is usually enough to deter a wise predator. Those who do attack risk a snout full of quills. The quills detach easily from the porcupine's skin; the barbed ends may work deep into the attacker's flesh, at times causing death.

The hollow quills provide buoyancy, and porcupines float high in the water when swimming and do not hesitate to swim wide streams or lakes.

Porcupines live about 18 years. ■

Dall's Porpoise
Phocoenoides dalli

Description: Dall's porpoises are black, with white belly and flanks. Often their dorsal fin is white-tipped, as are the two outer tips of their flukes.

Their tail stock has a hump that may serve as a keel to speed these swift swimmers through the water.

Dall's porpoises have 19 to 27 spade-shaped teeth on each side of their jaws and horny protuberances on the gums between their teeth that scientists think help the porpoises to grip squid, their chief prey.

The largest males grow to about 7 feet and weigh about 450 pounds; females are slightly smaller.

Range: Dall's porpoises occur in the North Pacific and adjacent seas from the Bering Sea south to Baja California.

(Patrick J. Endres)

In Alaska they move from the Gulf of Alaska to the Bering Sea in the spring and return in the fall.

Food: This species feeds on squid and fish such as suary, hake, herring, jack mackerel and bottomfish.

Life History: Dall's porpoises mature at ages 3 to 4. Breeding females produce a calf every year after an 11- to 12-month gestation period. Newborns are about 36 inches long and weigh about 85 pounds.

Frequently seen riding bow waves, Dall's porpoises are thought by scientists to be the fastest swimmers of all small cetaceans (whales, dolphins and porpoises). They travel alone or in small groups. Dall's porpoises may roll slowly at the surface, but they seldom jump clear of the water. They have a high metabolic rate and are not easily kept in captivity because of their excitable nature.

The species is named for American scientist William H. Dall, who became Acting Assistant of the U.S. Coast Survey in 1871.

Scientists estimate their life span at 20 years. ■

Harbor Porpoise
Phocoena phocoena

(John Hall)

Description: Nondescript animals lacking bold stripes or colors, harbor porpoises are black or dark gray on their back, grayish on their sides and white on their belly. A glimpse of their back, with the small triangular dorsal fin protruding slightly to the rear of center, is about all most people ever see of these animals.

They have a small, rounded head, and small, spade-shaped teeth, 23 to 28 on each side of the upper jaw and from 22 to 26 on each side of the lower jaw.

Smallest of North America's cetaceans, harbor porpoises reach a maximum length of between 5 and 6 feet, and weigh 120 pounds on average.

Range: Harbor porpoises range from the Arctic Ocean southward along the Pacific coast to southern California.

Food: This species feeds on a variety of small fish and squid.

Life History: Sexually mature at ages 3 to 5, harbor porpoises breed during summer. The cow gives birth to a calf 29 inches long and weighing 12 to 16 pounds after an 11-month gestation period.

Harbor porpoises may gather in schools of nearly 100 to feed, but are more often seen as singles, in pairs or in small groups. They often swim quietly at the surface, never ride the bow waves of a boat and are extremely shy. Despite their shyness, they will remain close to boat harbors. When a boat nears, the porpoises dive, only to surface when the boat backs off a few hundred yards. If undisturbed, harbor porpoises will continue to swim placidly, seemingly aimlessly, in the same general vicinity.

Studies of captive harbor porpoises have revealed that their underwater hearing sensitivity is among the highest ever measured.

This species is seldom displayed in aquariums because it is easily frightened, even when treated gently. They live an average of 13 years. ∎

Norway Rat
Rattus norvegicus

Description: Norway rats
are gray or reddish-gray, with
large, nearly naked ears. They
reach 15 to 16 inches, excluding
their 7- to 8-inch tail. Adults
weigh about a pound.

Range: Sailing ships brought
Norway rats to North America.
Whalers carried them to the
Pribilof Islands in the Bering

(Leonard Lee Rue III)

Sea in the mid-1800s. From there, they increased to such
numbers on one group of Aleutian islands that the group
became known as the Rat Islands.

This species is found in virtually all seaports in Alaska,
as well as in Fairbanks, Anchorage and in many other places
in the state inhabited by people. They depend on people's
carelessness with trash, waste food and dumps. Where people
keep their garbage buried, eliminate trash and there are no
hiding places, this species does not normally survive.

Food: Omnivorous, Norway rats eat fish, birds, insects,
garbage, grain, — almost anything edible.

Life History: This species becomes sexually mature at 2
months. Rats may produce six litters a year, are promiscuous
in their breeding and may breed at any time of year. From
four to 20 young make up a litter. They are born blind, deaf
and helpless, after a 21- to 30-day gestation period.

The Norway rats is generally a ground-dweller, building
extensive underground burrows to nest and store food.

Some rats have been documented to live to about age 4. ■

California Sea Lion
Zalophus californianus

Description: A coat sepia to dark brown when dry and black when wet, a prominent forehead, external ears, hind flippers that rotate forward and an overall slender body mark this species. Males lack the thickened neck of bull Steller sea lions.

Males average 8 feet and 800 pounds, females 5 feet and 250 pounds.

Range: Although the bulk of their population inhabits the California coast, this species ranges from Tres Marias Islands at about the latitude of Guadalajara, Mexico, north to British Columbia. They are being seen more frequently in Southeast and, rarely, in Prince William Sound. They prefer sandy or cobble beaches on the mainland close to the water and avoid offshore rocky islets frequented by Steller sea lions.

Food: California sea lions eat squid and octopus and a variety of finfish such as herring, Pacific whiting, rockfish, hake, salmon. They bring their prey to the surface, bite off its head and swallow the body whole.

Life History: Breeding occurs in July. Females come ashore usually in June to give birth, after an 11 1/2-month gestation, to their single pup that weighs about 13 pounds. They nurse their pups anywhere from six months to more than a year, depending on the food supply, the mother's health and age, the pup's sex and whether the female is ready to give birth to a new pup. About three weeks after giving birth, females seek out males who have established breeding territories, and mate. They then spend the rest of the time nurturing their pup. Males fast for the one to two

(Harry M. Walker)

months they defend their breeding territory. California sea lions, especially those inhabiting warmer climates, lose water to urination, panting and sweating. To counteract this water loss, adult males, particularly fasting individuals, sometimes drink seawater, a behavior called mariposa.

California sea lions are acrobatic animal performers. They were hunted almost to extinction in the 1800s for their oil, and later their hides, which were sold for 5 cents a pound for the manufacture of glue. Their whiskers were used for pipe cleaners. They received protection in 1909, but in the 1920s a lucrative trade in capturing young for the circus developed. They have now been protected for several decades and their numbers are increasing.

California sea lions have lived 18 to 20 years in captivity. ■

Steller Sea Lion
Eumetopias jubatus

(Jon R. Nickles)

Description: Steller sea lions are blond to dark brown and their coat has almost no underfur. They have a long neck, pointed head and tiny, but visible, ears. Their hind limbs are capable of forward motion and their front flippers are almost as long as the hind ones. Sea lions are remarkably agile. Even the largest bulls can climb rocks and ledges to haul out far above the water.

Sea lion bulls average 9 feet but can reach up to 13 feet in length, and weigh up to 2,400 pounds. Females are much smaller, 7 feet long and weighing 600 to 800 pounds.

Range: Steller sea lions occur in coastal waters from Dixon Entrance to the Pribilof Islands and north to St. Lawrence Island. They are found along the edge of the Bering Sea ice in winter, and haul out in the Pribilofs only during summer.

Some sea lions, particularly juveniles, wander throughout the North Pacific; individuals tagged in Alaska have been reported as far south as California.

Food: Sea lions eat a wide variety of foods including pollock, cod, rockfish, sculpin, greenling, sandlance, smelt, herring, salmon, halibut, flounder, octopus, shrimp and crab.

Life History: The breeding season begins in late May when mature bulls begin defending territories on their rookeries. The same rookeries are used year after year.

Females become sexually mature at 3 to 6 years and may produce young into their early 20s; males reach sexual maturity at 3 to 7 years but are not physically mature and able to defend a territory until about age 10. On large rookeries males generally have 14 to 17 females within their defended areas. Pups are born in late May and June, with most of the pupping taking place the first two weeks of June. Usually one pup is born; twins occur rarely. Average birth weight of the dark chocolate-brown pups is 44 pounds. Most females breed again within 7 to 10 days of giving birth.

Not all sea lions visit rookeries during the breeding season; many immature bulls and females without pups go to haul-outs, generally located adjacent to rookeries. In addition, some young males and pupless females may gather on hauling grounds where males defend territories and engage in breeding. Territoriality of bulls decreases about July 1; most breeding ceases by mid-July.

Pups are capable of swimming within hours of birth, but most remain on shore until they are 1 month old. In July cows swim near the rookeries with their pups; by late July bulls and cows without pups leave the rookeries.

Perhaps a quarter of adult females are barren each year, and mortality among pups is high, with perhaps half dying in their first year from malnutrition, drowning and predation.

Drastically declining populations of Steller sea lions in some areas of Alaska have scientists concerned. No specific cause has yet been determined, but lack of food for juveniles seems to be part of the problem. The Steller sea lion has been classified as "threatened" throughout its range under the Endangered Species Act, and the National Marine Fisheries Service is considering reclassification of the western stock as "endangered."

This species is named for George Wilhelm Steller, naturalist on Vitus Bering's 1741 voyage, who was the first to describe for science several animal species found in Alaska.

Females reach a maximum age of 30, males 20. ■

Harbor Seal
Phoca vitulina

Description: The hair of harbor seals varies from light gray with dark spots to nearly black with light markings. Lighter-colored seals predominate in the Gulf of Alaska, along the outer Kenai Peninsula and in the Kodiak archipelago. The percentage of darker seals increases farther south and west until the western Aleutians where dark seals predominate.

Harbor seals are earless, cannot rotate their hind flippers forward and cannot lift their belly from the ground when traveling on land. Each flipper has five claws to provide traction on land.

Males may reach 6 feet and weigh as much as 250 pounds, although their weight averages closer to 160 pounds. Females are about 25 percent lighter.

Range: The species occurs south to Mexico. In Alaska, harbor seals range from Kuskokwim Bay south along the coast to Southeast, and westward to the Aleutians and Pribilof islands. A freshwater colony inhabits Iliamna Lake. Harbor seals are generally found in nearshore waters and show strong site fidelity. However, recent tagging studies have shown that some seals may travel several hundred miles.

Food: Harbor seals eat a wide variety of fish and crustaceans, including herring, flounder, eulachon, salmon, rockfish, cod, sculpin, sandlance, octopus, squid and shrimp.

Life History: Breeding takes place in June or early July, with normally one pup born the following May or June. Newborns, about 35 inches long and weighing about 28 pounds, are weaned at about 4 weeks.

(Patrick J. Endres)

Pups are born with a short coat resembling that of their parents. A whitish, woolly coat, called lanugo, is normally shed *in utero*. Occasionally, a pup is born prematurely and still has its white coat.

Harbor seals were once the most common marine mammal within their Alaska range. In most parts of their range, such as Southeast and Bristol Bay, their populations appear to be healthy. However, in the northern Gulf of Alaska and Prince William Sound they have been declining for the last 15 to 20 years for unknown reasons.

Individuals are known to have lived in the wild for more than 20 years. ∎

Northern Elephant Seal
Mirounga angustirostris

Description: Adult northern elephant seals are light brown; immatures are gray. They are true, or earless, seals, with hind flippers that do not rotate forward. The male's snout hangs limply over his muzzle and is used to resonate when vocalizing. Females and young have a much smaller snout.

The largest of all seals in the northern hemisphere, males may reach 15 feet long and weigh 2 1/2 tons. Females are about 10 feet long and weigh about half a ton.

Range: Northern elephant seals congregate along the shores of Baja California, Mexico and California. Males routinely travel as far north as Southeast and the Aleutians for feeding.

(Frank S. Balthis)

Food: Elephant seals fast during pupping and molting periods. Otherwise, they eat mostly fish and invertebrates, sometimes at depths up to 3,000 feet. They swallow fish whole.

Life History: Great colonies of elephant seals once lived along the Pacific coast from California to Baja California. But because elephant seal blubber is almost pure oil and a big bull can yield more than 200 gallons of oil, which was considered superior even to that of sperm whale oil for lubricating machinery, the seals were butchered in great numbers. When hunting ended in the 1890s, few remained.

By the 1930s scientists counted about 500 seals, mostly in Mexican waters. Two decades later, wanderers from Mexico began swimming north into the species' original range. As their numbers increased under total protection, stragglers arrived in Alaska, with the first ones reported in the mid-1960s.

Pregnant cows arrive at hauling-out grounds on California's coastal islands and mainland in December, and within a few days bear a dark-haired pup after an 11-month gestation. The pup triples its weight or more within a month, when it is weaned.

The average life span for females is less than 20 years, males less than 10 years. ■

Northern Fur Seal
Callorhinus ursinus

(Harry M. Walker)

Description: Northern fur seals are dark gray to black with a lighter throat. Immature seals are glossy black above, washed with buff below. With durable, soft, silky fur overlaid with longer guard hairs, northern fur seals are renowned for their coat. So luxuriant is their coat in fact, that for nearly two centuries Russians and later Americans killed the northern fur seal for its pelt.

The webbed hind feet of northern fur seals can be turned forward, enabling these animals to move better on land than any of the true seals, and, like sea lions, they have external ears.

Males are 6 feet long, weigh 300 to 500 pounds, and occasionally to 700 pounds. Females are much smaller, about 48 to 50 inches long, and weigh about 75 to 100 pounds.

Range: About 80 percent of the world's northern fur seal population summers on the Pribilof Islands. However, in Alaska this species may be found in coastal waters from near shore to far off shore, as far north as, and including, Bristol Bay. Females forage 150 miles from the Pribilofs during summer breeding months.

Other rookeries occur on the Russian Commander Islands, in the central Kurils and on Robben Island in the southern Okhotsk Sea, and on San Miguel Island off California.

Females and young from Alaska winter along the slope between the continental shelf and the ocean floor as far south as California. Adult males may migrate with the main herd or winter in the North Pacific.

Food: Primarily fish eaters, northern fur seals consume squid, herring, saury, lanternfish, smelt, salmon, sandlance, shrimp, flounder, sole, turbot — altogether about 100 species of fish. They depend most heavily on schooling fish such as herring and smelt, and take relatively few salmon.

Life History: Adult males begin to arrive at Pribilof rookeries in May. A month later adult females arrive and form harems within territories established by harem masters. Fur seals between ages 2 and 6 arrive in June, and haul out in large groups separate from the harem areas. Yearlings do not arrive until fall and many remain at sea.

Females bear a single pup in late June or July, and breed again within about a week after giving birth. Females have

(Harry M. Walker)

a bifurcated uterus that alternates in producing offspring. The cow alternately nurses her pup and feeds offshore during summer. When she returns to the rookery and the thousands of wailing pups, she identifies her own pup apparently by its distinctive cry, for she will not nurse any but her own. Pups are weaned when the southward migration begins in October and November. Rookeries are empty by the end of December.

In the wild, northern fur seals live about 30 years at most. ■

Pacific Bearded Seal
Erignathus barbatus

Description: Bearded seals are gray to brown, and darkest along their back. Like other hair seals, they lack dense fur, and depend on a heavy layer of fat for warmth. They have exceptionally wide front flippers, their hind flippers cannot rotate forward and they have no external ears.

A tuft of stout, white whiskers, growing down each side of the muzzle give bearded seals their name.

Largest of western Arctic and Subarctic seals, bearded seal adults average 7 to 8 feet. Adult females may be slightly larger, but mostly the sexes are similar in size. Large adults may weigh more than 750 pounds in winter; from June through September adults weigh 475 to 525 pounds.

Range: Bearded seals generally are found in shallow waters to 660 feet over the extensive continental shelf of the Bering and Chukchi seas. In late winter and early spring they

(Lew Consiglieri, NMFS)

are found from the southern edge of the Bering Sea ice pack north to the solid pack ice, and are apparently most common south of Bering Strait. During summer and early fall they are most common along the edge of the polar pack ice in the Chukchi Sea, although some animals remain in open water during summer.

Bearded seals are not common in areas of unbroken, shorefast ice. In Alaska, they do not usually come ashore, although they do in other parts of their range. They occasionally swim into the lower Yukon and Kuskokwim rivers.

Food: Bearded seals eat a variety of marine invertebrates including shrimp, crab, clams, worms and octopus, and bottomfish. These **benthic** foods are widely dispersed over the Bering and Chukchi seas, and bearded seals are found anywhere with favorable ice conditions and water shallow enough for the seals to feed on the bottom. Bearded seals can dive for up to 20 minutes, and seem to prefer depths of 82 to 165 feet, but can dive as deep as 495 to 660 feet.

Life History: Males are sexually mature at age 6 or 7. Females first become pregnant at age 5 or 6, and have one pup at a time. Most pups are born from mid- to late-April. At birth they have a dense coat of soft, gray hair, which provides warmth. They shed this coat soon after birth. Newborns are large, weighing 70 to 80 pounds. They gain weight rapidly, mostly as they build fat, or blubber, and weigh about 190 pounds when they are weaned after only 12 to 18 days.

Bearded seals are reported to live about 30 years in the wild. ■

Ribbon Seal
Phoca fasciata

(Lew Consiglieri, NMFS)

Description: Adult ribbon seals can be recognized by banded coloration that gives the species its name. There are four nearly white bands, one around the neck, another around the rear end of the trunk, and one encircling each shoulder. The ribbon pattern is not visible in pups of the year, and becomes more recognizable as individuals approach sexual maturity. On adult males, the white bands contrast with a dark brown or black background. Width of these bands varies, and sometimes the bands coalesce. Adult females are similarly marked, but their ribbons are much less pronounced because of the lighter brown background.

They have very large, round eyes, and a short snout. Ribbon seals have inflatable air sacs off the end of the trachea that may provide flotation or be used in sound production.

Adult ribbon seals are more slender than other northern seals, and have a more flexible neck and foreflippers.

Adults of both sexes average about 5 feet in length and weigh from 175 up to 300 pounds. They lose weight in spring when they are basking on the ice and molting.

Range: Ribbon seal populations divide into two groups, the Okhotsk and the Bering-Chukchi populations. Little is known about exchange between these groups.

The Bering-Chukchi population concentrates in the central and western Bering Sea. In winter and early spring this population is most abundant in the northern part of the seasonal ice. Concentrations of ribbon seals can be located in the ice front zone during March through early June. In most years by the time the ice edge recedes north through Bering Strait, only a small number of ribbon seals still are associated with it. It is unknown where most ribbon seals go in summer. Some migrate north into the Chukchi Sea; others are pelagic in the Bering Sea.

Food: Ribbon seals feed on **demersal** fish and invertebrates including shrimp, squid, cod, sculpin, pollock, capelin, flat fish and eelpouts.

Life History: Males become sexually mature at ages 3 to 5, females between age 2 and 4. Breeding occurs in May, with a single pup born after an 11-month gestation period. Newborns, about 32 inches long, weigh about 22 pounds. A dense, white, woolly coat (lanugo) covers the pups except for their snout at birth. They shed the lanugo in six weeks, revealing a coat of short, sleek hair that is neither banded nor spotted, and is blue-gray on the undersides. Indistinct white bands begin to appear in some young ribbon seals as early as 12 weeks after birth, but the bands are usually not obvious until they molt at the end of their first year.

Ribbon seals can live to 30 years. ■

Ringed Seal
Phoca hispida

Description: Smallest of the light-colored northern seals, ringed seals resemble harbor seals, but have small rings on their coat from which they get their name. They are dark gray on top, lighter underneath. Breeding males have a dark face.

Ringed seals cannot rotate their hind flippers, a characteristic of earless seals. The first digit of their foreflipper is longer than any of the others. Strong claws on the front flippers are used to dig breathing holes in the ice and to make snow caves where the seals haul out to rest or have their pups.

Males average 4 feet and weigh 120 pounds; females are smaller.

Range: Ringed seals range widely throughout areas of seasonal and permanent pack ice, and have been reported

(S.C. Amstrup)

from all arctic areas people have visited, including the North Pole. They occur in greatest densities in the fast ice near shore where in winter they are the dominant seal species. They are also found far from shore in the pack ice. Ringed seals can dig and maintain breathing holes through 3 to 6 feet of ice so they do not depend on the movement of drifting ice for air holes.

Food: This species eats a variety of animals from several trophic levels. Zooplankton and arctic and saffron cod are particularly important. They also eat smelt, herring and shrimps.

Life History: Males mature sexually at ages 7 to 8; females at ages 6 to 7. Most breeding occurs in April and May, with a single pup born after an 11-month gestation period. The white-coated pups, about 23 inches long and weighing about 9 to 12 pounds, are born in snow lairs or in natural cavities in the shore ice or pack ice.

Weaning in ringed seals may occur somewhat later than for other ice-associated seals, at 4 to 7 weeks. However, information about weaning is poorly quantified. Ringed seal pups may dive soon after they are born, perhaps to escape predation by arctic foxes or polar bears. They molt their white pup-coat at about 4 to 6 weeks.

Pups spend their first few weeks in "subnivean" snow caves dug by the mother. These caves are 59 to 77 degrees F warmer than outside temperatures. While the pups are in these lairs, they dig many small "pup tunnels" and the lair may eventually expand to include 10 or more chambers and measure 40 feet or more in length. They remain unattended in their den while their mother is away feeding.

Records indicate individuals have lived to more than 40 years in the wild. ■

Spotted or Largha Seal
Phoca largha

(Lloyd Lowry)

Description: The coat of spotted seals typically has a pale silvery background, overlain along the dorsal surface of the nose, head and body by a darker, steel-gray wash or saddle. The entire coat is dappled with small, oblong, brownish-gray to black spots. Spotted seals are almost indistinguishable in appearance from harbor seals (*Phoca vitulina*). Spotted seals lack external ears, and their hind flippers cannot be rotated forward.

Large adult spotted seals of both sexes reach 5 feet and weigh between 200 and 300 pounds.

Range: Spotted seals occur in the Bering, Chukchi and Beaufort seas, depending on the season and condition of the ice pack. In winter and early spring they concentrate along the southern edge of the ice pack. As the ice retreats north, these seals move northward and shoreward. During summer, spotted seals haul out on sandbars and spits from Kuskokwim Bay to the Beaufort Sea, sometimes making extended trips to sea to feed. As freezeup begins in autumn, spotted seals in northern Alaska begin to migrate south.

Food: Spotted seals eat fish, crustaceans and cephalopods. Some of the most common prey species among the fish are capelin, pollock, herring, and arctic and saffron cod. They also eat shrimp, squid and octopus. Younger seals eat more crustaceans, older seals more benthic fishes such as flounders and sculpins.

Life History: Most breeding occurs in May. Pairs of spotted seals, or two adults and a pup, are seen frequently in May on flights over the southern ice front. Unlike their land-breeding relative, the harbor seal, spotted seals depend on the ice for breeding and pupping grounds.

Pups are born from late March to mid-April after a gestation period of about 10 1/2 months. At birth, pups have a long, whitish, woolly lanugo coat, which is shed two to four weeks later. The pups' first-year coat, after the lanugo is shed, resembles that of adults. Pups weigh between 21 and 26 pounds at birth, and are about 34 inches long. They are suckled about four weeks and triple their weight during this time.

Spotted seals are thought to be monogamous, at least for the season. Maximum longevity reaches at least 35 years. ■

Dall Sheep
Ovis dalli

Description: Although Dall sheep are generally white, individual coats may vary from snow-white through yellowish to brown, depending on dirt and stains. A few sheep have a dark tail or a few dark hairs in other areas of their coat, particularly individuals found on northeastern slopes north of the Alaska Range. The coat's hairs are brittle and hollow, and the coat may be 3 inches thick or more in winter.

(Tim Van Nest)

Both sexes of Dall sheep, the world's only white wild sheep, have golden-colored horns that range from light-honey color to dark brown. A ram's horns are heavy and curled, occasionally exceeding 40 inches in length. Ewes have thinner, straighter horns averaging 8 to 10 inches. Until about age 3, young rams are difficult to distinguish from mature ewes because of similar horn and body size. Growth rings on the horns indicate age.

Mature rams stand about 35 inches at the shoulder, ewes about 30 inches. Adult males weigh about 200 to 250 pounds, with some reaching 300 pounds. Ewes average 110 pounds and occasionally reach 150 pounds.

Range: Dall sheep are found in all major mountain ranges of Alaska, excluding Southeast. They also occur in Canada's

Yukon Territory and Northwest Territories, and a few inhabit northwestern British Columbia.

Food: Dall sheep obtain important nutrition from bunch grass and other grasses and sedges, dryas, willow and lichens, which, in winter, are exposed on wind-blown ridges. They also dig down through snow for food, but particularly deep snow and snow thickly covered with ice may prevent sheep from reaching food.

In spring, sheep follow the retreating snow line into the highest meadows and ridges, eating emerging succulents.

Life History: Dall sheep breed from late November through mid-December. Rams do not collect harems, but circulate freely among groups of ewes seeking receptive mates. Most fighting between rams takes place before the breeding season, and usually rams with the largest horns dominate. In many cases, rams substitute horn display for fighting to establish superiority.

Lambs of 5 to 6 pounds are born from mid-May through mid-June, after 175 to 180 days of gestation. By their first winter, young weigh 60 to 70 pounds.

Ewes mature sexually at age 1 1/2, but most don't give birth until age 3 or 4. They typically breed annually thereafter. Even old ewes, 13 to 15 years, give birth. Single births are the rule, and lambs have a low survival rate because of their harsh environment.

Dall sheep are intensely loyal to seasonal ranges, and may move as far as 20 to 30 miles between winter and summer range. Rams remain separate from ewes and lambs during late spring and summer, although both sexes may graze the same areas, and they often seek higher and more rugged terrain as summer progresses, possibly to escape insects and eat emerging vegetation. By October, both sexes begin to congregate on winter range, often a windblown slope where vegetation is easily accessible.

Predation, disease, accidental falls and avalanches kill some sheep, but winter climate exacts the greatest toll. Dall sheep must have escape routes near feeding areas, places where they can sprint to cliffs or rock outcrops to avoid predators. They are rarely seen where escape cover is lacking. Their survival also depends on cold winter temperatures and moderate snowfalls. Continued cold keeps snow light and

(Harry M. Walker)

powdery, while high winds remove snow from ridges, exposing food. Heavy, wet, freezing snow; rain on snow; or thawing and freezing cycles that produce icy slopes may spell starvation.

Although the proper name of this species is Dall's sheep, this guide will refer to them as they are commonly known, Dall sheep. The species is named for scientist William H. Dall, although it is unlikely he had anything to do with the sheep. Naturalist E.W. Nelson assigned the first scientific name to the species in 1884, *Ovis montana*, with a subspecies name of *dalli*. In 1897, J.A. Allen changed the species name from *montana* to *dalli*.

Most Dall sheep live at least 10 years; rams can live 20 years and ewes three or four years beyond that. ■

Shrews

Sorex species

Description: Small, highly energetic shrews are members of the family Soricidae, with worldwide distribution, and currently has nine representatives in Alaska, all members of the *Sorex* genus.

Most shrews are grayish-brown above with paler undersides. They have short legs, a long, pointed snout and long whiskers. Insectivores, shrews have tiny, sharp teeth because they are among the most ferocious of all carnivores. Musk glands emit a powerful odor that can deter other predators. They have poor eyesight but acute hearing and sense of smell.

The smallest of all mammals, shrews range in length from 3 to 6 1/2 inches, with a tail one-quarter to one-half

(Leonard Lee Rue III)

their length, and weigh from 5/100 to 7/10 of an ounce.

Range: Shrews are widely distributed in Alaska as the following list indicates:

St. Lawrence Island Shrew:	St. Lawrence Island
Pribilof Shrew:	St. Paul Island
Barrenground Shrew:	North Slope
Tundra Shrew:	Statewide, excluding Southeast
Common or Masked Shrew:	Brooks Range through Southeast
Dusky Shrew:	Brooks Range through Southeast
Water Shrew:	Yukon River to Southeast
Glacier Bay Water Shrew:	Southeast
Pygmy Shrew:	Statewide
Tiny Shrew:	Galena and Ruby on Yukon River, Susitna River Valley

Food: Shrews feed primarily on insects and small invertebrates. Some eat plant matter, and most eat any kind of meat, including each other. Western Alaska species will feed on blackfish in winter.

Life History: Breeding occurs from March to August. They produce several litters annually, each with two to 10 young born 17 to 28 days after breeding. Young are born naked and blind in a nest of grass and are weaned three weeks later.

Shrews are solitary, active year-round and spend much of their life scurrying under grass and leaf litter. They prefer moist to drier habitats and the water shrew is frequently found in marshes.

Most shrews live about one year. Maximum known life span for *Sorex* in the wild is 17 months.

Arctic Ground Squirrel
Spermophilus parryii

(Helen Rhode)

Description: The only ground squirrel species in Alaska, arctic ground squirrels are grizzled buff and gray on their upperparts, and buff to rusty on their underparts. Their nose, head and legs are rusty-buff.

The rounded head of the ground squirrel has a blunt nose and low, rounded ears. Short legs protrude from their robust body. Their tail, slightly more than one quarter of their total length, is flat and moderately bushy. Claws are long, slightly curved and quite strong.

This species grows from 14 to 18 inches, depending on their location within their range. Adults weigh about 2 pounds.

Range: Arctic ground squirrels are northern ground squirrels, members of the group known as Columbian ground squirrels, found from northeastern Hudson Bay, Canada, across the Arctic to northeastern Russia. They occur throughout much of Alaska in well-drained tundra from sea level to alpine areas. They do not inhabit the Yukon-Kuskokwim delta, Prince William Sound, Southeast and some offshore islands, but they are found in the Kodiak archipelago.

Food: Ground squirrels eat seeds, roots, bulbs, plant stems and leaves, mushrooms, insects, carrion and bird eggs.

Life History: Breeding occurs when the ground squirrels come out of hibernation. After 24 days, five to 10 naked, blind, toothless young are born, weighing about 24/100 ounce each. Within 2 weeks their weight increases to more than an ounce. At 3 weeks their eyes open. They nurse for about a month, then leave their burrow to feed on green vegetation. After 5 or 6 weeks they leave their natal burrow and set up a new home, usually in an abandoned burrow in the colony.

As winter approaches, arctic ground squirrels prepare a sleeping chamber, grass-lined and several inches in diameter, and perhaps 5 to 8 feet underground. When they enter hibernation, they curl into a tight ball and their body temperature gradually drops. In Alaska, arctic ground squirrels hibernate from September or October to April or May.

Arctic ground squirrels are sometimes known as parka or parky squirrels in Alaska.

Males can live about 6 years, females more than 11 years. ■

Northern Flying Squirrel
Glaucomys sabrinus

Description: A small, nocturnal tree squirrel, this species is reddish, cinnamon or snuff-brown above, pale pinkish or whitish below. It has large, dark eyes, a fur-covered membrane extending from front to rear legs on each side, and a horizontally flattened tail. The membrane enables it to glide from perch to perch, but it cannot truly fly like birds or bats.

Northern flying squirrels reach 12 to 15 inches, and weigh 3 to 5 ounces, depending on their location. Animals in Southeast are smaller and lighter than those elsewhere.

Range: This species occurs in interior, southcentral and southeastern Alaska where forests are sufficiently dense to provide suitable habitat.

(Dr. Robert Dietrich)

Food: Northern flying squirrels eat mushrooms, fungi, lichens, seeds, fruits, buds, eggs, nestlings and carrion.

Life History: Mating occurs from March to late June, depending on the weather. Females bear one litter annually, usually of two young, between May and early July. Alaska is the northernmost extension of their range. Flying squirrels living farther south can have larger litters.

For nesting sites, northern flying squirrels require old growth forest or mixed forest that includes some old growth trees where the trees have plenty of cavities or where clumps of witches broom are common. Far more sociable than red squirrels, the only other common tree squirrel in Alaska, colonies of flying squirrels may live together in groups of five to 20 in one nest or tree cavity. During the coldest weather, they move from cavities to brooms where they huddle together in a state of torpor.

Individuals probably have a home territory of only about 20 acres, and remain within that area for life, unless hunger or predator pressure forces them to move. To escape predators, northern flying squirrels need a forest, preferably of conifers, with trees close enough that they can glide from one to another.

Four is about the maximum age limit for northern flying squirrels. ■

Red Squirrel
Tamiasciurus hudsonicus

Description: Alaska's only species of tree squirrel, red squirrels appear basically rusty red on top; their sides may be olive-gray or reddish, lightly sprinkled with black. Their grayish-white undersides have some hairs tipped with black. A white ring encircles each eye.

These small squirrels have a flat, bushy tail; fairly long ears and fairly long pelage that is soft but not silky.

Red squirrels grow to about 12 inches and weigh 8 ounces.

Range: This species occurs throughout most of Alaska where spruce grow, especially along rivers. They are not found north of the Brooks Range, on parts of the Seward Peninsula, on the Yukon-Kuskokwim delta or on the lower part of the Alaska Peninsula.

Food: In Alaska, red squirrels eat primarily spruce seeds, but they will vary their diet with spruce buds, berries, fungi, insects, larvae, eggs and young birds.

Life History: Mostly solitary, red squirrels defend their territory vigorously except during breeding season. Sometimes a litter may remain together for a time, but eventually the siblings separate and each establishes a territory.

Red squirrels usually breed during February or March, and young arrive about a month later. They are blind and naked at birth, and totally dependent on their mother until they are about one-third grown. Litters range from three to seven and nests are commonly in tree cavities or in leaves.

Red squirrels may have several nests within their range, and may shift from one to the other frequently. Home range is usually one-half to one acre, and the resident squirrel

(Tim Van Nest)

seldom leaves this area.

Red squirrels build a food cache, most commonly spruce cones in Alaska, around a rock, log or group of trees. Within a few years, a food cache is an obvious landmark in a squirrel's territory, with feet-deep piles of cone bracts where a squirrel has cut them from cones and removed the seeds.

Red squirrels remain active all winter. They burrow in their nests during storms and deep cold, but they move about their territory during most winter days.

Records indicate red squirrels can live for at least 7 years in the wild, 10 years in captivity. ■

Vole or Meadow Mouse
Microtus species

Description: In summer, *Microtus* are brown to gray above and gray underneath. Their feet are gray and their tail is darker on top than underneath. In winter, they become grayer.

(Leonard Lee Rue III)

These medium-sized, robust-bodied voles have long, loose fur and a comparatively short tail covered with short hairs. Their short, well-haired ears do not project much beyond their fur. Although their legs are normal length for this type of animal, they sometimes appear unusually short because of the length of their body hair.

Voles are land mammals, but they are adept at swimming and diving.

Range: Even though the range of some *Microtus* is not well-defined, the following *Microtus* species are listed for Alaska.

Microtus pennsylvanicus, (Meadow Vole):
Range: The Carolinas to Alaska. Total length: 3 1/2 to 5 inches; tail makes up about half that length. Weight: 2 1/2 ounces.

Microtus oeconomus, (Tundra Vole):
Range: Alaska, northwestern Canada, Eurasia. Total length: 5 inches. Weight: 3 ounces.

Microtus longicaudus, (Long-tailed Vole):
Range: Eastern Alaska to Mexico. Total length: 7 to 8 inches. Resembles *pennsylvanicus* but tail is longer, ears larger and

coat grayer. *Microtus coronarius*, formerly a separate species, is now included with this species. Weight: 1 to 2 ounces.

Microtus xanthognathus, (Yellow-cheeked Vole):
Range: Northwestern Canada and Alaska, from central Alberta north to the arctic coast and west to central Alaska. Total length: to 9 inches. Weight: 4 to 6 ounces.

Microtus miurus, (Singing Vole):
Range: Alaska and northwestern Canada. Total length: 6 inches. Weight: 1 to 2 ounces.

Microtus abbreviatus (Insular Vole):
Range: St. Matthew and Hall islands in the Bering Sea. *M.a. fisheri* is found on St. Matthew, *M.a. abbreviatus* on Hall. Total length: 5 to 7 inches. Weight: 1 1/2 to 2 1/2 ounces.

Food: *Microtus* voles eat primarily grasses, seeds and flowers and they sometimes eat their weight in vegetation in a 24-hour period. The insular vole feeds on tufted hairgrass, arctic dock, round-leaf willow and roseroot.

Life History: *Microtus* voles adapt their appearance, diet and life history to their environment. The meadow vole, the most widespread, may give birth year-round in temperate climates. In Alaska, breeding commonly stops during cold weather, and probably two to four litters are produced annually, depending on weather.

Females mate when less than a month old, and after a period of 21 days give birth to five to eight or more per litter. Young, born blind and deaf, are hairless at birth and depend on their mother and each other for warmth. Young begin to grow hair within 12 hours and within four days are covered with fine hair.

At 2 weeks, young feed themselves and gain weight rapidly. In the meantime, the mother, who breeds again to the first male she encounters, is carrying another litter.

Voles are not long-lived. Although records indicate that many only live a few months, some individuals in the wild are known to have lived for up to 1 year. A captive *Microtus* lived for almost 4 years. ■

Red-backed Vole
Clethrionomys rutilus and
Clethrionomys gapperi

Description: Red-backed voles usually have a broad reddish stripe down the center of the back and buffy-red sides. Their underparts are pale-buff, their tail brownish above, grayish-buff below and black-tipped. These small- to medium-sized voles have small eyes, and small ears reaching just above their fur.

Counting their 1 1/2-inch tail, their total length is 5 1/2 inches. They weigh about 1 to 1 1/2 ounces.

Range: Northern red-backed voles range from Malaspina Glacier at least as far north and west as Norton Sound on the Bering Sea coast and northward to Barrow. They are found on Unimak Island in the Aleutians and on St. Lawrence Island in the Bering Sea. They are not found on the Kodiak archipelago or on Nunivak Island in the Bering Sea. Southern red-backed voles, *Clethrionomys gapperi*, occur on the mainland of Southeast and on some islands in Southeast but are absent from Admiralty, Baranof and Chichagof islands.

Food: This species is omnivorous but eats chiefly greens, berries, seeds, lichens, fungi, insects and carrion. They are cannibalistic.

Life History: Breeding begins in late winter or early spring and continues to late fall. Two to eight young are born after a gestation of 17 to 19 days. Nest are elaborate grass-lined cavities under rocks, logs or other shelters close to the ground.

Red-backed voles are found mostly in cool, damp localities, and are partial to forests. They can usually be distinguished from meadow mice (*Microtus*), which they resemble, by their

(Doug Murphy)

usually conspicuous reddish back. Other distinguishing characteristics include the close, soft fur, longer ears and more slender body.

Best places to find red-backed voles are near old logs or in mossy, overgrown areas. They are active day and night, and usually do not occur in large colonies, as does *Microtus*.

Though they prefer the forests, red-backed voles are sometimes found on the tundra, and in open fields adjacent to forests. They are active all winter, and tunnel about the snow, moving as freely in winter as in summer.

Members of this genus have been known to live 4 years. ■

Pacific Walrus
Odobenus rosmarus

Description: Short, sparse fur covers the pink-to-cinnamon-brown skin of walrus. An individual's color lightens when it enters the water, gets cold and its blood vessels constrict. The skin wrinkles or folds about the base of the flippers, on the sides and on the belly. Adult bulls have numerous large bumps in the skin of their neck and shoulders to provide "armor" when they joust with other males.

(Harry M. Walker)

(Greg Syverson)

Bulls and cows sport long, white, ivory tusks — actually elongated upper canine teeth. Bulls normally have thicker, heavier, straighter tusks.

Walrus are related to seals but are more robust and less streamlined, with a thick, heavy neck. Like sea lions and fur seals, walrus can rotate their flexible hind flippers forward, allowing good maneuverability on land or ice. Both males and females have broad muzzles with short, heavy bristles. Adult males and females can be identified by the shape of their head; the male's head is more square and blocky.

Walrus have air sacs in their upper neck. These bladders can be filled with air to support the head at or above the water's surface when an individual needs to sleep while in the water. These bladders may also aid vocalization. Walrus emit a variety of noises including one resembling that of church bells.

Mature bulls reach 10 to 12 feet or more, females to 8 or 9 feet; bulls may weigh more than 2 tons, cows often exceed 1 ton.

Range: Pacific walrus are found in the Bering and Chukchi seas. Most winter in the seasonal ice pack of the Bering Sea, with the greatest concentration, mostly females and young,

10 to 150 miles southwest of the western end of St. Lawrence Island.

As the ice recedes north in April, May and June, most walrus move with it to summer in the pack ice of the Chukchi Sea.

Thousands of adult males remain in the Bering Sea, hauling out on the Walrus Islands in Bristol Bay and on islands in Russia's Gulf of Anadyr.

Southward movement of the main herd from the Chukchi into the Bering Sea occurs in October, November and December.

Food: Walrus feed mainly on bottom-dwelling invertebrates, including clams, snails, crabs, shrimp and worms. They occasionally eat seals. A walrus's mouth is well-adapted to sucking up bottom-dwellers. They have a narrow mouth with an unusually high roof; strong, thick lips not deeply cleft along the side of the face; and a thick, pistonlike tongue.

Life History: Breeding occurs in February and March, but the fetus doesn't begin to grow until about mid-June. Calves, dark gray-brown and weighing 85 to 140 pounds, are born in late April or early May on the northward migration. Calves depend on their mother for at least 18 months, some for much longer. Most cows do not breed again until the year following the birth of their last calf, resulting in a three-year interval between young.

Walrus can live to 35 in the wild. ■

Least Weasel
Mustela rixosa

*(M. Andera, American
Society of Mammalogists)*

Description: Dark brown
upperparts and light underparts, both of which turn white
in winter, characterize least weasels. In all seasons, the tip
of their short, stubby tail contains only a few black hairs
among brown or white ones. By contrast, the tail tip of short-
tailed weasels remains distinctly black throughout the year.

Much smaller than short-tailed weasels, least weasels
average 8 to 10 inches in length and weigh 3 ounces.

Range: Least weasels are found throughout Alaska except
for offshore islands of the Bering Sea, Aleutian Islands west
of Unimak, the Kodiak Island group and most islands of
Southeast. They are sparsely distributed throughout their

range except along the Arctic Slope where they become abundant, especially when rodent numbers are high.

Food: This species preys primarily on mice and voles, secondarily on birds, fish, small mammals, insects and worms. Least weasels have a high metabolism and hunt day and night because they eat 40 percent or more of their body weight daily.

Life History: Least weasels reach sexual maturity in their second summer. They breed in mid- to late summer but because of delayed implantation, most young are not born for eight to 10 months. More southerly least weasels do not always undergo delayed implantation and may produce up to three litters in one season. A litter contains three to 10 young and if food is plentiful, most will survive. Both parents care for young, which are fully grown by fall and set out on their own.

Least weasels make their dens, with side chambers to store their excess kills when rodents are plentiful, in rodent burrows, stumps, rock outcroppings and under old buildings.

The life span of the least weasel is unknown. ■

Short-tailed Weasel or Ermine

Mustela erminea

(Barbara Willard)

Description: In summer, short-tailed weasels appear uniform chocolate brown above and yellowish-white below. In winter their short, soft fur becomes snow-white, leading to the name ermine, but their tail tip remains black year-round.

Short-tailed weasels have a long, thin body, short legs and a pointed head. Being members of the Mustelid family, weasels have an anal gland that can produce a strong odor to deter predators. They grow to 14 to 16 inches long, and weigh about 7 ounces.

Range: This species occurs throughout Alaska except on

(Lon E. Lauber)

offshore islands of the Bering Sea and the Aleutian Islands west of Unimak.

Food: As master predators, weasels live entirely off the prey they kill, which includes microtine rodents, shrews and mice. They also eat birds, eggs, young hares, pikas, insects and fish. Their high metabolism propels them to consume nearly half their weight daily in food.

Life History: Breeding usually occurs during an individual's second summer. Delayed implantation arrests the egg's development and young are not born until the following May or June. Three to 10 young are born in a den in a hollow log, in a burrow or in a hollow tree. The availability of food in the mother's home territory influences the number of young that are born. Young stay in the den until they are 30 to 45 days old, when they begin to hunt with their mother. Weasels commonly live in old cabins, where they quickly eliminate all mice.

The life span of the short-tailed weasel is unknown. ■

Baird's Beaked or Giant Bottlenose Whale

Berardius bairdii

Description: White blotches often occur on the undersides of these slate-gray to brown whales whose skin usually shows many scratches. They have a narrow snout that resembles a bottle neck, and in adult males the lower jaw extends well past the tip of the upper jaw. Two pairs of teeth erupt from the tip of the lower jaw in adult males.

(Illustration by Donald Sineti)

The longest known male specimen measured 39 feet and weighed about 13 tons. Females are larger, and have been recorded at 42 feet and 14 tons. Males average 34 feet and 10 tons, females 37 feet and 12 1/2 tons.

Range: This species occurs in the Bering Sea from about the latitude of St. Matthew Island south through passes in the Aleutians to about the latitude of Japan and southern California in the Pacific.

Food: Baird's beaked whales eat deep-water fish, squid and octopuses.

Life History: Little is known about this toothed whale species. Mating occurs in the spring, and a calf, about 15 feet long and weighing a ton, is born in midwinter after a 17-month gestation period.

Leonard Stejneger named the species in 1881 for Spencer Fullerton Baird (1823-1887), an American zoologist and naturalist who became secretary of the Smithsonian in 1870 and U.S. Commissioner of Fish and Fisheries in 1871.

Scientists project a life span of 70 years for this species. ■

Beluga or Belukha Whale
Delphinapterus leucas

Description: The only all-white whales, belugas are blue-gray to brownish as newborns and lighten to all white by their fifth or sixth year. Their robust body tapers to a neck region and a small head relative to body size. Their dorsal fin is replaced by a narrow ridge serrated laterally to form a series of small bumps, which may be visible on close view but often appears smooth from a distance. These small toothed whales have 40 to 44 conical-shaped teeth.

Males average 13 feet and 3,300 pounds, females 12 feet and 3,000 pounds.

Range: Belugas occur throughout the Arctic Ocean and Bering and Chukchi seas. An isolated stock inhabits Cook Inlet.

(Leslie Nakashima)

Considered shallow-water whales, belugas are most often seen in bays, inlets and rivers. They have been seen in Lake Iliamna and 600 miles up the Yukon River.

Food: Belugas eat fish, squid, crustaceans and marine invertebrates. They find prey by well-developed echolocation.

Life History: Females reach sexual maturity at age 5, males at age 8. Breeding occurs in May, and after a gestation period of 14 1/2 months, a calf about 5 feet long and about 100 pounds is born.

Relatively slow swimmers, belugas usually move at less than 6 or 7 knots, but can sprint to 14 knots.

Residents of coastal Alaska from Cook Inlet to the Arctic have traditionally hunted belugas for meat, **muktuk** (maktak) and oil. A commercial beluga fishery was attempted in Cook Inlet during the 1930s. A large net spanned Beluga River, and whales entering the river at high tide were trapped. The operation ceased after about 100 whales were killed.

Growth layers in the teeth of belugas set their maximum life span at about 35 years. ■

Blue Whale
Balaenoptera musculus

Description: The bluish-gray coloration of blue whales is
punctuated by irregularly shaped, random, light gray
markings, mostly on the undersides but commonly extending
up the sides. The color varies, with young tending to be
lighter. The underside of the **flukes** is white. Diatoms
covering the **ventral surface** may form a thin, yellowish
coat, giving blues their nickname, "sulphur bottom."

A single, small dorsal fin, about one-third of the way
forward from the tail is a handy identification marker.
Their flukes generally remain submerged when they are at
the surface, and may remain so even as they dive, hindering
identification because most experts rely on the blow and
flukes for positive identification.

The blow of these whales lasts up to five seconds, and on
a windless day, a fully grown blue whale can shoot its vapor
25 to 30 feet high in a shape resembling an inverted
teardrop.

Blue whales are the largest animals ever known to have
lived. They can grow to 100 feet and weigh 200 tons with a
45-foot girth, although their average size is 85 feet and 100
tons. An elephant could stand on the floor of a blue whale's
mouth without touching its upper jawbone. A blue's stomach
can contain two tons of food. Its heart may weigh half a ton,
and may pump up to 12 tons of blood through its body. The
tongue of blue whales may weigh 4 tons, more than the total
weight of an elephant.

Range: Blue whales feed in offshore waters throughout
the Gulf of Alaska and into the Bering Sea in summer; they
return to tropic and subtropic waters in winter.

Food: These leviathans feed on **krill**, especially

euphausiids, which they strain from the water with their 3-foot-long **baleen**, or whalebone, plates. Scientists estimate blue whales eat four tons of food per day during summer.

(Larry Wade)

Life History: In summer, blue whales feed in northern waters. In winter they breed off western Mexico, and at an unknown location in warm waters of the North Atlantic or Caribbean Sea.

Adults mature sexually at about 10 years. Every two or three years females give birth during winter after an 11- or 12-month gestation period. Calves are weaned at 7 months, after they have gained an average of 7 to 8 pounds an hour throughout their entire suckling period. Calves may measure 24 feet at birth, and reach 50 feet and weigh 23 or 24 tons when they are weaned.

Steam whalers with harpoon guns just about wiped out blue whales in the early 20th century. The species has been protected since 1965 by nations that signed the International Whaling Convention.

Their average life span is estimated to be 80 years. ■

Bowhead Whale

Balaena mysticetus

(Jack W. Lentfer)

Description: Bowhead whales have a white area several feet long on their chin and tail that contrasts with their overall dark color. They have no dorsal fin. Their head, with its highly arched upper jaw, takes up more than one-third of their total length

Bowheads reach 50 to 60 feet in length and weigh about a ton per foot. Their baleen is finely fringed and very long, with some plates dangling 12 feet or more. Females are usually bigger than males.

Range: Bowheads inhabit waters of the northwestern and northern Bering Sea, the Chukchi Sea and the Arctic Ocean. They winter near the ice front in the southwest Bering Sea in Russian waters, then swim north with the ice through Bering Strait starting in April, and summer in the Arctic Ocean as far east as Canada's Banks Island.

Food: These whales eat almost anything that their baleen plates can enmesh: **amphipods**, euphausiids and various crustaceans, all of which are known collectively as krill.

Life History: Bowheads achieve sexual maturity between ages 12 and 20. They breed in arctic waters during summer and give birth to a 10- to 15-foot-long calf in spring after a gestation period of 12 to 16 months. A cow has one calf every three to seven years.

When migrating, bowheads swim at about 4 knots, and normally dive for less than six minutes. Wounded whales have been reported to have remained submerged for at least 56 minutes.

Bowheads are named for the resemblance of their strongly curved jaw to the shape of an archer's bow. This species was found by commercial whalers in 1849 and generated profits for the whalers for the next 60 years. Bowheads provided more baleen than any other baleen whale species, an average of 1,500 pounds per animal, plus about 100 barrels of oil, which fueled household lamps.

Northern nations have protected bowheads from commercial hunting since 1935, although Natives are allowed to kill bowheads each summer under a quota system.

The probable life span of the bowhead is in debate. For some years, scientists pegged the figure at about 40 years. However, discovery of stone harpoon points in recently killed bowheads has led to speculation that bowheads may live much longer because, according to some accounts, this type of stone point has not been used in about a century. ■

Cuvier's Beaked or Goosebeak Whale

Ziphius cavirostris

Description: A tan to reddish-brown body with a lighter head and neck and scarred skin identifies this species. Its robust body sports a small, curved dorsal fin, small flippers, a small notch in the middle of the flukes and a single pair of V-shaped throat grooves. A pair of conical teeth pro-trude from the gum line at the tip of the lower jaw in males.

(Illustration by Donald Sineti)

Males average 20 feet and 4 tons, slightly larger females 21 feet and 5 tons.

Range: Although Cuvier's is another of the open-ocean beaked whales about which science knows little, it is distributed worldwide in temperate and tropical waters. In Alaska, it has been reported as far north as the Bering Sea.

Food: Cuvier's eat primarily squid and deep-water fish and invertebrates.

Life History: No specific breeding season has been deter-mined. A single calf may be born any time during the year.

These whales frequently occur in groups of from 10 to as many as 25. They have been reported to jump free of the water, and when they begin a deep dive, they often raise their flukes out of the water and dive nearly vertically. They have been known to stay submerged for more than 30 minutes.

This species is named for French naturalist and educator Georges Cuvier (1769-1832), one of the founders of comparative anatomy and vertebrate paleontology.

Cuvier's have been known to live to 36 years. ■

Fin or Finback Whale
Balaenoptera physalus

Description: The dark gray or black back and sides contrast with the creamy-white undersides. Two light-colored chevrons, which begin at the back midline behind the blowhole and extend obliquely down the sides toward the tail, help identify this species.

Asymmetrical pigmentation characterizes the baleen and lower jaw. The first third of baleen plates on the right side are cream-colored, the remainder are blue-gray; skin on the lower lip is light on the right side, dark on the left.

Fin whale baleen, 375 plates on each side, hangs up to 3 feet from the upper jaw.

Fins are slightly smaller, more slender and have a more V-shaped head than do blues. The slightly back-curved dorsal fin extends 14 to 24 inches out from the last third of their back and appears shortly after the blow in a diving animal. Their blow, 18 to 20 feet high, normally occurs once per minute between dives that vary from 2 to 28 minutes,

(Bev Agler)

(Kim Robertson)

but average 10 to 15 minutes.

Second largest of the world's whale species, fin whale females grow to 80 feet and weigh up to 70 tons.

Range: Fin whales are found as far as the ice pack in summer, and migrate toward, but do not reach, tropical waters in winter. Some individuals remain in subpolar waters, where food is more abundant, even in winter. Fin whales may be seen off Alaska's coast as far north as Point Hope in summer, and as far north as the Aleutians year-round.

Food: Fin whales eat mainly krill, but also feed on anchovies, **capelin**, herring, **lanternfish** and other small fish, as well as squid.

Life History: Adults are sexually mature at ages 6 to 12. Cows produce a calf every two or three years after a gestation period of 11 to 12 months. Newborns measure about 20 feet and weigh almost 2 tons.

Among the fastest whales, fins can swim up to 20 knots and dive to 1,000 feet. Unlike blue and sei whales, with which they are most often confused, fin whales sometimes leap clear of the water. They surface obliquely so that the top of the head breaks the surface first. After blowing, they arch their back, rolling forward to expose their dorsal fin but rarely showing their flukes.

Scientists peg the average life span of this species at 100 years. ■

Gray Whale
Eschrichtius robustus

Description: Gray whales are mottled gray overall. Their head, appearing narrow and sharply pointed when viewed from the front, is often covered with barnacles in front of the blowhole. Gray whales lack a dorsal fin but have a number of bumps or knobs and a ridge down their **dorsal surface**. They have 150 pairs of thick, creamy-yellow baleen plates about 15 inches long.

Gray whales average 42 feet and 33 tons.

Range: In the eastern Pacific, gray whales spend June through October feeding in the Chukchi, Bering and Beaufort seas, then migrate up to 6,000 miles south to breeding lagoons along the west coast of northern Mexico.

Formerly, gray whales were known in the western North Pacific from the Sea of Okhotsk to southern Korea, and in the North Atlantic. Korean gray whales were overhunted between 1899 and 1933, primarily by Japanese whalers, and this stock is now thought to be extinct.

(John Kroeger)

Food: While in northern waters in the summer, gray whales stock up on food by dredging through ocean bottom mud to feed on amphipods. They apparently do not feed but live off their blubber during their southward migration. Individuals may lose about one-fifth of their weight while on their wintering range south of San Francisco.

Life History: Mating occurs in winter and cows give birth in about 13 months. Calves are weaned in July. Adults do not reach sexual maturity until they are ages 5 to 7.

Pregnant females leave Alaska waters in September, swimming southward at 5 mph, arriving in the vicinity of Baja California in December. Calves, born in shallow lagoons, head north with their mothers in early March.

Gray whales are a coastal-inhabiting, bottom-feeding species with one of the longest migrations of any mammal. Usually fewer than 10 gray whales migrate together, but 1,000 or more will crowd into a 30-mile breeding lagoon during summer.

Gray whales reach full size by age 40, and their life span has been known to reach at least 69 years. ■

Humpback Whale
Megaptera novaeangliae

Description: Humpbacks are basically black with a white region of varying size on their belly, which on close examination often may be cross-hatched with thin dark lines. The normally white flukes are deeply notched in the center, and scalloped on the rear margin. Their nearly all-white flippers grow to 14 feet, about a third as long as the body.

(Harry M. Walker)

Their small dorsal fin, located slightly more than two-thirds of the way back on the back, varies in size and shape from a small, triangular nubbin to a substantial, sickle-shaped fin. The dorsal fin frequently includes a step or hump, visible when individuals arch their back to dive, and from which the species derives its common name.

A humpback's bushy blow reaches from 8 to 10 feet.

Unlike other baleen whales that have bony ridges, humpbacks have fleshy knobs or protuberances randomly distributed on the top of their head and lower jaw. They are particularly susceptible to parasites and their head, flippers and flukes are frequently covered with patches of acorn and stalked barnacles and other marine crustaceans. Up to a half ton of barnacles may be attached to a single humpback.

Female humpbacks average 49 feet and 35 tons; males average 46 feet and 25 tons.

Range: Humpbacks range throughout the southeastern Bering Sea, the Aleutians, Prince William Sound and Southeast in spring, summer and fall. In winter they swim south at least as far as Banderas Bay on the Mexican coast, the tip of Baja California and the Hawaiian Islands. Some animals may remain year-round in Southeast.

Humpbacks also occur in the Atlantic. Apparently humpbacks worldwide divide into two or three major populations, which do not mix.

Food: Humpbacks feed primarily on krill, and small fish such as herring, sardines, anchovies and capelin.

Life History: In the Northern Hemisphere, humpbacks mate between October and March and calve after a gestation period of 12 to 13 months. At birth the calf measures 16 feet, and weighs about 2 tons.

Unusually acrobatic as whales go, humpbacks can be seen breaching, creating huge splashes when they fall back into the water, and commonly show their flukes when diving, thereby exposing the white underside and rippled rear margin that enables scientists to identify individuals.

Observers in Alaska have seen humpbacks corral a school of herring, following which the whale dives to come up through the school, mouth agape, scooping in a huge meal.

Humpbacks are thought to live about 50 years. ∎

Killer Whale or Orca

Orcinus orca

Killer whale and Dall's porpoise. (Eva Saulitis)

Description: Killer whales are black with extensive areas of white on their undersides and oval patches of white on the sides of their head. Most animals have a light gray saddle mark just behind their dorsal fin and white on the undersides of their flukes. Both all-black and all-white killer whales have been reported.

This species is easily distinguished by its dorsal fin that, in adult males, is extremely erect and may be as long as 6 feet. Though the fin of females and immature males is less than 3 feet tall, it is still taller than that of any other whale species and is distinctly sickle-shaped and pointed at the tip.

Killer whales have 10 to 12 large teeth on each side of each jaw.

Adult males average about 26 feet and 8 tons, but some may reach 30 feet and weigh 9 or 10 tons; females average 23 feet and 4 tons.

Range: Killer whales range worldwide. In Alaska they are most abundant in the Aleutians, but have been recorded from the Beaufort Sea south throughout the state's coastal waters. They are common in the Gulf of Alaska, Prince William Sound and Southeast.

Food: A diverse diet sustains these skilled killers that are known to have eaten prey ranging from birds and turtles to larger whales. There are at least two genetically separate stocks of killer whales, transients and residents. Transients are known to eat mammals, while residents are fish-eaters. Japanese who examined the stomach contents of 364 killer whales found in order of occurrence: fish (cod, flatfishes, sardines, salmon, tuna and other species); octopus and squid; dolphins; whales and seals. U.S. Department of Commerce officials reported the following stomach contents of 10 orcas killed between Kodiak Island and southern California: three California sea lions, four Steller sea lions, seven elephant seals, two harbor porpoises, two Dall's porpoises, one minke whale, one halibut, two sharks and a squid.

(Jon R. Nickles)

Life History: Killer whales don't reach sexual maturity until ages 10 to 15, but once they reach that age, they breed and give birth year-round. Newborns are about 8 feet long and weigh about 400 pounds. They are capable of swimming alongside their mother immediately and are nursed when the mother turns on her side and squirts milk into their mouth by muscular contraction. Their milk has six times as much protein as human milk.

Killer whales travel in groups; herds of 150 have been reported although usually the group is much smaller. Resident pods, or groups of whales, are matrilineal, i.e., a female will travel with both her male and female offspring, even when the offspring become adults. Adult bulls wander off to breed with females from other matrilineal groups.

Among the fastest of whales, they can swim at 25 knots or more. They have no natural enemies other than man and can live 40 to 50 years in the wild. ■

Minke or
Little Piked Whale
Balaenoptera acutorostrata

Description: A black to dark gray dorsal surface contrasts with the white on their belly and on the underside of their flippers. A diagonal band of white appears on each flipper and parts of the underside of their flukes may be bluish-gray.

Like fin whales, minkes sometimes have a chevron on their back behind their head. They often have two regions of light gray on each side, one just above and behind the flippers, another just in front and below the dorsal fin.

The baleen, typically 8 inches long, is mostly yellow-white with fine, white bristles; up to half of the rear plates may be brown or black.

One of the most distinct features of minkes is their extremely narrow, pointed head with a single, central head ridge. Their dorsal fin, tall and sickle-shaped, protrudes from the rear third of their back. Their blow is small and inconspicuous.

Smallest of the Northern Hemisphere's baleen whales, minkes may reach approximately 30 feet and weigh up to 9 tons. Males average 26 feet and 6 tons, females 28 feet and 8 tons.

Range: In the eastern North Pacific, minkes occur from the Chukchi Sea south to northern Baja California during summer, and from central California south to central Mexico during winter. They favor icy waters more than other baleen whales except the bowhead and gray.

Food: Minkes feed on krill, and on fish such as herring, mackerel, cod and whiting.

Life History: At 6 years, minkes reach sexual maturity. They breed year-round; females produce a calf every one

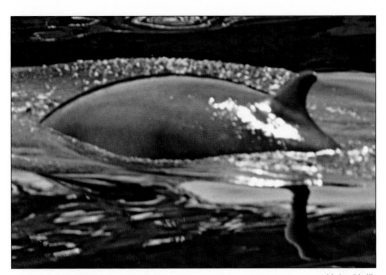

(John Hall)

to two years after a 10- to
11-month gestation period.
Newborn calves are 10 feet long and weigh 1,000 pounds.

Frequently seen as single animals, pairs or trios, minkes
may congregate in areas of abundant food in the northern
seas during spring and summer. They are more likely to be
seen close up than larger whales because they often approach
boats, particularly stationary ones. Minkes also swim close
to shore and enter bays and inlets. Among the fastest
swimmers, they can move at 18 to 24 knots. They sometimes
leap clear of the water and re-enter smoothly, head first, or
with a big splash like humpback whales.

By the 1970s, minkes had become the most heavily hunted
baleen whale worldwide.

Scientists estimate minkes live to 47 years in the wild. ■

Narwhal

Monodon monoceros

Description: Young narwhals are uniformly dark bluish-gray on the back but rapidly develop the numerous leopardlike spots — the result of white mottling on a dark gray or blackish background — on their back and sides characteristic of adults.

A dorsal ridge replaces the dorsal fin in narwhals.

These mammals have only two teeth. In females these

(Fred Bruemmer)

teeth rarely emerge from the gums although instances
have occurred where one or two tusks have been exposed.
In males, one and sometimes both teeth protrude from the
snout, spiraling counterclockwise. The purpose of the tusk
is unknown, but most scientists think it is a secondary sex
characteristic, like the antlers of deer or the inflatable snout
of the bull elephant seal.

Males grow to about 16 feet and weigh about 3,500
pounds; females are slightly smaller.

Range: Narwhals inhabit the Arctic Ocean and adjacent
seas. They occur commonly in the Canadian Arctic and
northwestern Greenland. Although rare in Alaska waters,
they have been reported as far west as Nelson Lagoon on
the Alaska Peninsula.

Food: Narwhals feed on deep-living crustaceans, squid,
polar cod and Greenland halibut.

Life History: Narwhals give birth to 5-foot calves during
summer in the Arctic Basin. Ice forces them south in winter,
and in Canada they reach Hudson Bay and Labrador.

Narwhals get their name from the Norwegian word for
"corpse whale," for their mottled skin resembles that of a
drowned human.

Individuals may live to about 40 years. ■

Northern Right Whale
Eubalaena glacialis

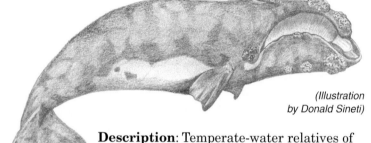

(Illustration
by Donald Sineti)

Description: Temperate-water relatives of bowhead whales, northern right whales are black or slate gray, usually with irregular-shaped white patches on their undersides. Right whales sport rough, fleshy bumps on their snout, or bonnet, in front of their blowholes. These wartlike areas, which scientists call callosities, shelter crustaceans that hitch rides on the whales.

Like the bowheads, right whales have no dorsal fin. They skim through the water when feeding, rather than gulping, so they don't hold tremendous amounts of water in their mouth like the blue or humpback does. Their 230 baleen plates measure 6 to 9 feet.

From a distance, right whales can be identified by their distinctive double spout, exhaled through two well-separated blowholes. They average 40 to 50 feet and, like bowheads, weigh about a ton per foot of length.

Range: This species was distributed historically throughout the northern temperate oceans. Though highly endangered, some right whales have been seen off the Washington, Oregon and California coasts in recent years. All photo-documented sightings of this species in the North Pacific should be reported to officials.

Food: Right whales feed on krill, including small **copepods** about the size of a match head, and on euphausiids.

Life History: Scientists are uncertain about the breeding habits of this species, but speculate they breed early in the year in temperate waters and give birth after a year-long gestation.

After whalers nearly exterminated them, northern right whales were given worldwide protection in 1935. The species has not recovered and its population levels are now critically low.

Scientists are uncertain about the life expectancy of this species. ■

Sei Whale
Balaenoptera borealis

Description: Sei (pronounced "say") whales are steel gray on the back, sides and tail end of the underside. Their flippers and flukes lack the white underneath of blue and fin whales. Also unlike the fin, their right lower lip and mouth are uniformly gray. Fine, grayish-white fringes protrude from the uniformly grayish-black baleen.

The snout is less pointed than that of fin whales, and appears slightly arched when viewed from the side. The sickle-shaped dorsal fin, from 10 to 24 inches long, is located about two-thirds of the way down the back, farther forward than on blue and fin whales.

The blow of seis shoots upward at least 15 feet and is cone-shaped with the small end pointing down.

Sei females average 49 feet and 17 tons; males average 46 feet and 14 tons. North Pacific sei whales appear to be smaller than those of the southern hemisphere, which has produced seis measuring 60 feet.

Range: Sei whales are widely

(Jerry Wheaton, courtesy Stephen Leatherwood/NOSC)

distributed in all oceans, but seldom are found near pack ice. In summer, seis range from the Aleutians south to the latitude of California's Channel Islands.

Food: Sei whales are skimmer feeders and usually do not dive deeply. In the northern part of their range, they feed on copepods. In the rest of their range, their food is more varied and includes krill and a variety of small schooling fish.

Life History: Sexually mature after age 10, seis breed in winter and produce a single calf every three years after a gestation of 11 to 12 months.

Seis usually are found singly, in pairs or small groups. Reputed to be the swiftest of the great whales, seis normally cruise at 6 to 8 knots and can speed to at least 23 knots. Some whalers have reported bursts to 30 knots from a harpooned sei.

Seis are closely allied to fin whales, but somewhat less common. Norwegians named this species because the whales sometimes arrive on their coasts at the same time as the *sei*, or pollock.

Scientists estimate their life span at about 60 years. ■

Sperm Whale
Physeter macrocephalus

Description: Sperm whales, whose body excluding the head appears corrugated or shriveled, are usually dark gray with a lighter area on their belly and forehead. Their skin is white around their mouth.

These whales have a distinct dorsal hump, usually rounded, about two-thirds of the way back from the tip of their snout. Immediately behind the hump, a series of knuckles are clearly visible when the whale arches its back before diving. The broad, triangular flukes are deeply notched in the center of the rear margin, and are almost always raised when diving.

The single blowhole of sperm whales is well to the left of the midline and far forward on the head. The small, bushy blow, usually less than 8 feet, emerges forward and to the left of the head. Sperm whales have a huge head, from a fourth to a third of their total length depending on sex, with males having the higher proportion. Their blunted, square snout may project up to 5 feet beyond the top of their narrow lower jaw.

The enormous, boxlike head of sperm whales may contain three or four tons of spermaceti, a liquid wax valued as a lubricant for fine machinery. At one time sperm oil was the finest fuel for lamps, and made fine smokeless candles. Early whalers thought this material was the animal's sperm, hence the name.

Scientists have long speculated on the function of spermaceti. It may aid the whale in echolocating by focusing and reflecting sound. It may serve as a cooling agent, decreasing the whale's buoyancy during prolonged dives.

Sperm whales are likely the world's deepest-diving mammals. Using hydrophones, scientists have tracked a diving sperm whale to a depth of 8,200 feet. Two bulls were

(Edward Steele)

killed off South Africa in water nearly 2 miles deep; both had been submerged for 80 minutes and had fresh, bottom-dwelling sharks in their stomachs.

Males reach 50 feet or more and weigh 40 tons; females 36 feet and 22 tons.

Range: Males are found in Southeast, the Gulf of Alaska, the Aleutians and into the Bering Sea. They generally prefer deep water and remain well offshore. Females and young stay in warmer water to the south.

During winter, males migrate south and breeding groups gather off the continental slope of California and Mexico. Sperm whales are polygamous, and some battles occur between males during breeding season.

Food: Sperm whales eat chiefly squid, preferring giant squid but also eating 30- to 40-inch squid, and cuttlefish.

Life History: Females mature sexually at ages 8 to 11; males at about 19. The 14- to 16-month gestation period produces a calf about 13 feet long and weighing 1 ton. Calves nurse for about two years.

The maximum known age for sperm whales is 77 years. ■

Stejneger's or Bering Sea Beaked Whale

Mesoplodon stejnegeri

Description: This species is dark gray-brown with a lighter belly and skin marked by scarring. Males have a single pair of broadly flattened teeth placed well back and protruding upward from their lower jaw, which is longer than the upper. They have small flippers and a small, curved dorsal fin.

Adults average 16 feet long and weigh more than 1 ton.

Range: This species ranges throughout the Gulf of Alaska and into the lower half of the Bering Sea. They have been reported as far south as Monterey, Calif.

Food: Stejneger's beaked whales eat squid and deep-sea fish.

Life History: Little is known of this species. Carcasses that washed ashore in Cook Inlet, the Gulf of Alaska and the Aleutians have provided scientists with some of their few opportunities to study these whales.

(Lon E. Lauber)

The species is named for Leonhard H. Stejneger (1851-1943), who was born in Norway and came to the United States in the 1880s. He went to work at the Smithsonian Institution, where he became curator of the department of biology in 1911. Stejneger was renowned for his work with birds, amphibians and reptiles.

Members of this genus are known to have lived 27 years. ■

Gray Wolf
Canis lupus

(Patrick J. Endres)

Description: Wolves vary greatly from almost pure black to nearly white, with many shades of gray between. Other wolves are brown or yellow, some have reddish tinges to their coat. Wolves in southern Alaska are darker and slightly smaller than those in the Arctic.

Most adult males in Alaska weigh 85 to 115 pounds, with

particularly large individuals reaching 145 pounds. Females are smaller and rarely weigh more than 110 pounds. Wolves reach their adult weight at about age 1.

Range: Excluding *Homo sapiens* (man), no other terrestrial mammal species has a greater natural range than does the wolf. They occur in a variety of habitats throughout Alaska except for the Aleutians beyond Unimak, the Prince William Sound area and Admiralty, Baranof and Chichagof islands in Southeast.

Food: Wolves are skilled predators and will prey on whatever animals are available including moose, caribou, deer, Dall sheep, mountain goat, snowshoe hare, beaver, salmon, waterfowl and mice and other small mammals. There are also reports of cannibalism.

Wolves hunt in packs, but they do not kill prey daily. They may take a large prey every few days in winter; in summer several days may pass with wolves eating little. Wolves are more likely to hunt old, injured and sick prey, but with deep snow or other favorable conditions, wolves can take prey in its prime.

Life History: Wolves live in packs that usually include the parents and the current year's pups. Sometimes packs include several females and their young. Pack size may range from two to 30; six or seven is about average. Females usually breed when 22 months old, giving birth to an average of four to seven pups in late May to early June after a gestation period of 60 to 66 days. Litters vary from two to 13 pups, with mature females usually producing the largest litters. Females ordinarily bear a litter every year.

Both parents care for the young. Pups and adults leave the den site in midsummer and by fall they may travel considerable distances. All the while, adults are teaching the pups to hunt. The youngsters are not able to kill large game for themselves until late winter when they have reached adult size.

Scientists speculate that wolves can live to at least age 16. A wild female has been documented to have reached age 13 3/4. ■

Wolverine
Gulo gulo

Description: Glossy dark brown fur marked with two pale lateral stripes converging at the base of the skunklike, bushy tail characterizes these burly, big-footed members of the weasel family. Their broad head is grizzled gray, with a black muzzle, short ears and dark, beady eyes. Wolverines have a low-slung body with powerful legs and long, curved claws.

Wolverines weigh 15 to 45 pounds and reach 3 to 4 feet,

(Tom Soucek)

and stand 15 to 18 inches at the shoulder. Their maximum weight is probably about 50 pounds. Females are smaller than males. The wolverine is the largest land-dwelling member of the weasel family; the sea otter, roughly twice the wolverine's size, is the largest member of the family.

Range: Wolverines are found throughout mainland Alaska and on some islands of Southeast.

Food: Omnivorous wolverines will eat anything they can from blueberries to moose. Their body is designed for scavenging and they feed heavily on carrion; sometimes a number of wolverines gather to feed on a beached whale or sea lion. They also take small mammals such as voles, squirrels and hares.

Wolverines are too short-legged to be fast runners, hence they cannot ordinarily catch a wary moose, caribou, sheep, or goat. They apparently do surprise some prey, and once they leap onto or get their teeth into a small ungulate (hoofed mammal), they can kill it. Although they are remarkably strong for their size, their reputation for ferocious attacks on big carnivores is overdone. They do vigorously defend their food, but they go out of their way to avoid bears, wolves and other large predators.

Life History: Breeding occurs in May, June and July with kits born in January through April. The number of young depends on the availability of food, and in years of low food supply, no kits will be born even if mating is successful. Kits emerge from dens in snow caves, hollow stumps, under rock piles or in abandoned beaver houses in early summer and remain with the mother until fall.

Solitary hunters, wolverines patrol a tremendous area in their quest for food, 240 square miles for adult males, for example. Still, starvation figures importantly in the mortality rate of wolverines.

This species lives about 5 to 7 years in the wild, but there are records of individuals reaching ages 12 and 13.

Woodchuck
Marmota monax

Description: Woodchucks, reddish above and tawny to hazel below, have long, coarse hair with shorter, softer underhair. A heavy-set body; short, flattened, well-haired tail; a broad head with a blunt nose; low, rounded ears and small eyes characterize these burrowing mammals known variously as woodchucks, marmots or groundhogs. Their rudimentary thumb has a flat nail and their strong claws are adapted for digging.

Woodchucks grow to about 20 inches and weigh 6 1/2 to 16 1/2 pounds.

(Leonard Lee Rue III)

Range: This species occurs locally in eastern interior Alaska between the Yukon and Tanana rivers and from around Fairbanks east to the Yukon border.

Food: Woodchucks feed mainly on plants, grasses, forbs, fruits, grains and legumes, with insects thrown in once in a while.

Life History: Breeding occurs in spring, often with snow still on the ground. About four weeks later, females give birth to from two to six blind, helpless young. Their eyes open at 4 weeks, at which time they begin to emerge from the den to feed on green vegetation.

By midsummer, the mother drives all or some of the young from the den. The young then take up residence in nearby dens or dig their own den.

Woodchucks are generally solitary, although at times a pair will occupy the same burrow and several individuals might gather at a favorite feeding spot.

Woodchucks prefer open woodlands, thickets near fields and clearings. They spend much of their lives hibernating — up to nine months a year in northern-dwelling individuals — and dig burrows with two or three, sometimes more, emergency exits. A mound at the entrance consisting of excavated soil from the tunnel characterizes all woodchuck dens. Although primarily a ground-dwelling mammal, they can climb trees and are good swimmers.

Woodchucks can live to 13 to 15 years. ■

Bushy-tailed Woodrat
Neotoma cinerea

Description: Bushy-tailed woodrats are gray to tawny on their back and sides with white, buff or pale gray on the underparts and feet. Their long, bushy tail is dark above, lighter below. They have large ears and eyes and long, soft hair.

Woodrats grow from 9 to 19 inches in total length and weigh from 7 ounces to 1 pound; females are smaller than males.

(Robert Hahn)

Range: Southeast is apparently the northern end of this species's range. They have been found from White Pass south on the Alaska mainland.

Food: Bushy-tailed woodrats are primarily vegetarians, eating a variety of seeds, shoots, berries, nuts and roots. Occasionally they eat invertebrates.

Life History: Males maintain a harem of from one to three females and will vigorously defend their harem from other males. In Alaska, this species produces one litter annually of from one to four young, with two the average, after a gestation of 24 to 39 days. Bushy-tailed woodrats are generally solitary, and although ranges may overlap, each den usually shelters only one adult.

A woodrat's nest is a mass of sticks surrounding a nest woven of soft grasses, shredded bark, rags or whatever is available. The nest may be in a cliff crevice, in a tree or in a cave. An average nest may be 4 or 5 feet across, but some are much larger. Their nests contain items that the animals have carried off or traded from a cabin or camp, such as bits of broken glass, coins, buttons, foil. Anything shiny, glittery or strange seems to attract them.

A related species of the bushy-tailed woodrat lived for 7 3/4 years in captivity. ∎

Where to See Mammals

Many accessible areas of Alaska are renowned for their varied wildlife. Other places draw visitors because they have a few species in abundance. Either way, Alaskans are proud of their wildlife and encourage others to enjoy the mammals that make Alaska special.

Red fox kits. (Greg Syverson)

Below is a list of some of the more accessible places in Alaska to see mammals.

Hyder: Brown and black bears when the fish are running in Salmon Creek.

Anan Creek: Black bear.

Pack Creek, Admiralty Island: Brown bear. An Alaska Department of Fish and Game permit is required to visit Pack Creek.

Glacier Bay National Park: Mountain goat. Bear. Harbor seal. Porpoise. Killer and humpback whales. Marine mammals, including sea lions, seals and humpback whales, cruise Icy Strait just outside the park.

Cordova/Copper River Delta: Wolf. Beaver. Muskrat. Members of the weasel family. Harbor seal, Steller sea lion, sea otter and whales offshore.

Resurrection Bay and Kenai Fjords National Park: Sea otter, harbor seal, Steller sea lion. Whales. Mountain goat.

Seward Highway along Turnagain Arm: Dall sheep. Beluga whales when fish are running.

Anchorage: Moose. Red squirrel.

Eklutna Lake Valley: Dall sheep. Mountain goat. Red fox. Lynx. Porcupine. Snowshoe hare. Hoary marmot. Short-tailed weasel. Collared pika. Voles.

Steller sea lions. (Harry M. Walker)

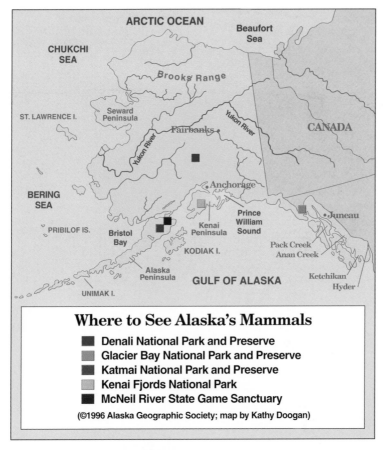

Where to See Alaska's Mammals

- ■ Denali National Park and Preserve
- ■ Glacier Bay National Park and Preserve
- ■ Katmai National Park and Preserve
- ■ Kenai Fjords National Park
- ■ McNeil River State Game Sanctuary

(©1996 Alaska Geographic Society; map by Kathy Doogan)

Denali National Park: Moose. Caribou. Dall sheep. Grizzly. Marmot. Red fox. Beaver. Wolf, if you're lucky and keep your eyes open. Visitors to Eielson Visitor Center in Denali National Park are likely to meet the ground squirrel greeting squad that patrols the bluff on which the center sits. The National Park Service has installed signs at squirrel eye level to discourage visitors from feeding these friendly critters because an overweight ground squirrel has difficulty escaping predators.

Richardson Highway between Paxson and Delta Junction: Bison.

Chena River State Recreation Area: Snowshoe hare.

Dalton Highway: Dall sheep. Grizzly. Red fox. Arctic fox. Muskoxen.

Brown bear. (Don Pitcher)

Katmai National Park:
 Brown bear. Moose.
 Porcupine. Weasels.
Kodiak Island Group: Brown bear. Sitka black-tailed deer.
 Red fox. Weasels. Steller sea lion. Harbor seal. Sea otter.
 Whales.
McNeil River State Game Sanctuary: Brown bear. Red
 fox. Open by permit only during height of bear-viewing
 season. Apply to Alaska Department of Fish and Game by
 March 1 for permit. Permits are awarded through a lottery.
Pribilof Islands: Northern fur seals. Arctic foxes usually
 enchant people who are fortunate to witness their antics.

Mountain goats. (Mike Jones)

In the Pribilof Islands, the foxes will approach to sniff packs, cameras and other human possessions. Food and small items should be safely stored, and as with all wild animals, it is best to observe them from a distance.

Alaska Zoo: The zoo in south Anchorage has a collection of northern species.

Musk Ox Farm: The farm in Palmer in Southcentral raises muskoxen and is open to the public. ■

Moose. (Greg Syverson)

Glossary

Amphipod: A marine crustacean, usually 1 to 2 inches long, whose body has been compressed sideways to give it a shrimplike appearance. Most amphipods are transparent or gray but they vary from brown and red to green or blue-green.

Annulation: A ringlike part of the anatomy.

Baleen: Also known as whalebone. Whalebone refers to the hundreds of strips of baleen, a flexible, bonelike material, that hang from the gum of the upper jaw of baleen whales. These strips are fringed, and the fringes act as strainers to capture krill. Once the strainers fill with krill, whales force water back out through the sides of their mouth, swallowing the food that remains. Baleen was used most commonly as stays for women's corsets.

*Gray whale baleen.
(Therese L. Hoban)*

Benthic: Associated with the bottom of the ocean.

Bugling: The call of the bull elk during mating season.

Capelin: A smeltlike fish.

Copepod: A large group of freshwater and marine crustaceans. Marine varieties make up a major portion of the pelagic marine food web.

Demersel: Associated with the bottom of the sea.

Dorsal Surface: The upperside or back of a whale. The dorsal fin is the single fin located along the back of some whales.

Euphausiids: Shrimplike marine invertebrates, 1 to 3 inches long.

Humpback fluke. (Bruce Wellman, courtesy Charles Jurasz)

Fluke: The expanded flat portion at the tip of a whale's tail.

Krill: A food source for whales. Krill is usually associated with euphausiids but more and more the term is taking on the general meaning of food, especially for baleen whales.

Lanternfish: A group of small, deep-water fishes found only in the Pacific Ocean that are fluorescent. These fish are of no commercial interest because they are so small that they slip right through the openings of a commercial net. Some species of lanternfish are known to occur as far north as the Bering Sea.

Muktuk: The skin and outer layers of a whale. This can consist of several layers from the body of a bowhead or beluga whale, including the outer skin, a layer of flesh just below the outer skin and a layer of blubber of varying thickness.

Ventral Surface: The underside or lower surface of a whale. ■

Additional Reading

Banfield, A.W.F. *The Mammals of Canada*. Toronto: University of Toronto Press, 1977.

Burns, John J., Kathryn J. Frost and Lloyd F. Lowry. *Marine Mammal Species Accounts*. Fairbanks: Alaska Department of Fish and Game, 1985.

King, Judith E. *Seals of the World*. Second Edition. Ithaca, New York: Comstock Publishing Associates, a division of Cornell University Press, 1983.

LaRoe, Edward T., Project Director. *Our Living Resources, A Report to the Nation on the Distribution, Abundance, and Health of U.S. Plants, Animals, and Ecosystems*. Washington D.C.: National Biological Service, U.S. Department of the Interior, 1995.

Lentfer, Jack W. Ed. *Selected Marine Mammals of Alaska, Species Accounts with Research and Management Recommendations*. Washington, D.C.: Marine Mammal Commission, 1988.

MacDonald, Stephen O. and Joseph A. Cook. *The Mammals of Southeast Alaska, A Distribution and Taxonomic Update*. Fairbanks: University of Alaska Museum, 1996.

Neff, Nancy A. *The Big Cats, The Paintings of Guy Coheleach*. New York: Harry N. Abrams, Inc., 1982.

Nowak, Ronald M. *Walker's Mammals of the World*. Fifth Edition, 2 Volumes. Baltimore and London: The Johns Hopkins University Press, 1991.

Riedman, Marianne. *The Pinnipeds: Seals, Sea Lions and Walruses*. Berkeley: University of California Press, 1990.

Wooding, Frederick H. *Wild Mammals of Canada*. Toronto, Montreal, New York: McGraw-Hill Ryerson, 1982.

Wynne, Kate. *Guide to Marine Mammals of Alaska*. Fairbanks: Alaska Sea Grant College Program, 1993.

The **ALASKA GEOGRAPHIC** Library

The Alaska Geographic Society is a non-profit, educational organization dedicated to improving geographic understanding of Alaska and the North. Each year The Society publishes four *ALASKA GEOGRAPHIC®* books full of information and colorful photographs, each book focusing on a particular geographic region or resource-related topic. The Society has published nearly 90 high-quality books since its founding in 1968; of these, the nearly 60 titles listed below are available today.

Members receive a subscription to *ALASKA GEOGRAPHIC®* quarterly as part of their annual society membership. In addition, these award-winning, informative books are sold in bookstores and specialty shops worldwide.

Other benefits for Alaska Geographic Society members include a valuable 20 percent members discount, which can be applied to purchases of *ALASKA GEOGRAPHIC®* back issues and other books published by The Society, as well as an assortment of top-quality merchandise, such as videos, maps and gift items, available through The Society. To learn more about these other items, or for current membership rates, write or call for our complete catalog. To order any of the books listed below, see instructions on page 175.

■ ■ ■

Admiralty: Island in Contention, Vol. 1, No. 3. A review of Southeast's Admiralty Island: its geology and historical past, its present-day geography, wildlife and sparse human population. 78 pages, $19.95.

Richard Harrington's Antarctic, Vol. 3, No. 3. Canadian photojournalist Harrington takes readers through the remote regions of the Antarctic and Subantarctic. More than 200 color photos. 104 pages, $19.95.

The Silver Years of the Alaska Canned Salmon Industry: An Album of Historical Photos, Vol. 3, No. 4. This issue commemorates the heyday of the salmon canning industry from the late 1800s to 1970s with text and more than 450 historic photos. 168 pages, $19.95.

Alaska Whales and Whaling, Vol. 5, No. 4. A look at Alaska's whales, their life cycles, travels and travails, and whaling in the North. Includes a fold-out poster of 14 whale species in Alaska. 144 pages, $19.95.

Aurora Borealis: The Amazing Northern Lights, Vol. 6, No. 2. Dr. S. I. Akasofu of the University of Alaska, Fairbanks, a leading expert on the aurora, explains in simple terms what causes the aurora, how it works and how and why scientists are studying it. With index; 96 pages, $19.95.

The Stikine River, Vol. 6, No. 4. Route to 1800s gold strikes, the Stikine is the largest and most navigable river flowing from Canada through Southeastern Alaska and to the Pacific. With fold-out map; 96 pages, $19.95.

Alaska's Great Interior, Vol. 7, No. 1. An overview of the region between the Alaska and Brooks ranges, including Fairbanks, its economic hub; area rivers; communities and history. With fold-out map; 128 pages, $19.95.

Alaska National Interest Lands, Vol. 8, No. 4. Reviews each of Alaska's national interest land selections (d-2 lands), outlining their location, size and access and briefly describing special attractions. 242 pages, $19.95.

Alaska's Glaciers, Vol. 9, No. 1. (Revised 1993) Examines glaciers in-depth, their composition, exploration, distribution and scientific significance. With diagrams, color and historical photos. With index; 144 pages, $19.95.

Islands of the Seals: The Pribilofs, Vol. 9, No. 3. Herds of northern fur seals and flocks of seabirds drew Russians to these remote islands where they founded permanent communities. 128 pages, $19.95.

Alaska's Oil/Gas & Minerals Industry, Vol. 9. No. 4. Experts detail the geological processes and resulting mineral and fossil fuel resources that contribute substantially to Alaska's economy. 216 pages, $19.95.

Adventure Roads North: The Story of the Alaska Highway and Other Roads in The Milepost, Vol. 10, No. 1. From Alaska's first highway, the Richardson, to the famous Alaska Highway (Alcan), this issue reviews Alaska's roads and the country they cross. 224 pages, $19.95.

Anchorage and the Cook Inlet Basin, Vol. 10, No. 2. An in-depth review of this commercial and urban center of Alaska. Heavily illustrated with color photos; comes with two fold-out posters and one map. 168 pages, $19.95.

Alaska's Salmon Fisheries, Vol. 10. No. 3. A comprehensive look at Alaska's most valuable commercial fishery, including a district-by-district tour of salmon fisheries throughout the state. 128 pages, $19.95.

Up the Koyukuk, Vol. 10, No. 4. A thorough exploration of the vast drainage of the Koyukuk River, third largest in Alaska. 152 pages, $19.95.

Nome: City of the Golden Beaches, Vol. 11, No. 1. Reviews the colorful history of one of Alaska's most famous gold rush towns. Includes nearly 200 historical black-and-white photos. 184 pages, $19.95.

Alaska's Farms and Gardens, Vol. 11, No. 2. An overview of the past, present and future of agriculture in Alaska, with a wealth of information on growing fruits and vegetables in the Far North. 144 pages, $19.95.

Chilkat River Valley, Vol. 11, No. 3. Explores the mountain-rimmed valley at the head of the Inside Passage, including the huge numbers of bald eagles that congregate there each year. 112 pages, $19.95.

Alaska Steam, Vol. 11, No. 4. The inspiring history of the Alaska Steamship Co. and the pioneers who navigated the hazardous waters of the northern travel lanes to serve the people of Alaska. 160 pages, $19.95.

Northwest Territories, Vol. 12, No. 1. A detailed look at Canada's immense Northwest Territories, site of some of the most beautiful and isolated land in North America. With fold-out map; 136 pages, $19.95.

Alaska's Forest Resources, Vol. 12, No. 2. A close look at the economic, botanical, and recreational value of Alaska's forests. Includes a section on identification of the state's 33 native tree species. 200 pages, $19.95.

Alaska Native Arts and Crafts, Vol. 12, No. 3. Offers an in-depth review of the art and artifacts of Alaska's Native people. Artwork is illustrated in more than 200 color photos. 216 pages, $24.95. (In stock Summer, 1997)

Our Arctic Year, Vol. 12, No. 4. Vivian and Gil Staender's simple, compelling story of their year in the wilds of Alaska's Brooks Range, with only birds, nature and an unspoiled landscape. 150 pages, $19.95.

Where Mountains Meet the Sea: Alaska's Gulf Coast, Vol. 13, No. 1. First-hand descriptions of the 850-mile arc of coastline stretching from Kodiak to Cape Spencer at the entrance to the Inside Passage. 192 pages, $19.95.

Backcountry Alaska, Vol. 13, No. 2. A full-color look at Alaska's remote communities, including how to get there, what to do and where to stay. 224 pages, $19.95.

British Columbia's Coast, Vol. 13, No. 3. A look at Canada's gold coast and the Canadian portion of the Inside Passage, including the scenic Queen Charlotte Islands. With fold-out map; 200 pages, $19.95.

Dogs of the North, Vol. 14, No. 1. Examines the development of northern dog breeds and evolution of sled-dog racing, including the internationally known Iditarod Trail Sled Dog Race. 120 pages, $19.95. **LIMITED SUPPLY.**

Alaska's Seward Peninsula, Vol. 14, No. 3. This issue chronicles the blending of the Eskimo culture with the white man's search for gold. With fold-out map; 112 pages, $19.95.

The Upper Yukon Basin, Vol. 14, No. 4. A description of the remote area surrounding the headwaters of one of the continent's mightiest rivers and gateway for Alaska's early pioneers. 120 pages, $19.95.

Dawson City, Vol. 15, No. 2. Author Mike Doogan relates the colorful history of the Klondike gold rush and takes a look at Dawson City today. Historical and contemporary photos. With index; 96 pages, $19.95.

Denali, Vol. 15, No. 3. Provides an in-depth look at the 20,320-foot crown of the Alaska Range, its lofty nieghbors and surrounding parklands and wilderness areas. With fold-out map and index; 96 pages, $19.95.

The Kuskokwim River, Vol. 15, No. 4. Reviews one of Alaska's most important rivers, from its headwaters in the Kuskokwim Mountains to its mouth on Kuskokwim Bay. With fold-out map and index; 96 pages, $19.95.

Katmai Country, Vol. 16, No. 1. This issue examines the volcanic world of Katmai National Park and Preserve and adjoining Becharof National Wildlife Refuge.With fold-out map and index; 96 pages, $19.95.

North Slope Now, Vol. 16, No. 2. This issue brings readers up to date on the economic and political forces that have shaped the North Slope. With fold-out map and index; 96 pages, $19.95.

The Tanana Basin, Vol. 16, No. 3. A review of this urban center of interior Alaska. Includes reviews of the lifestyle and history of this portion of Alaska's heartland. With fold-out map and index; 96 pages, $19.95.

The Copper Trail, Vol. 16, No. 4. This issue examines the Kennecott copper deposits, Copper River & Northwestern Railway, Cordova, southeastern Prince William Sound. With fold-out map and index; 96 pages, $19.95.

The Nushagak River, Vol. 17, No. 1. Reviews this important corridor, and details the lifestyle and resources of this site of one of the world's largest commercial fisheries. With fold-out map and index; 96 pages, $19.95.

The Middle Yukon River, Vol. 17, No. 3. Follows the course of the Yukon from Fortymile, near the Canadian border, down river to Holy Cross. With fold-out map and index; 96 pages, $19.95.

The Lower Yukon River, Vol. 17, No. 4. From Holy Cross, this issue traces the serpentine route of the Yukon through its braided delta to the mouth on the Bering Sea. With index; 96 pages, $19.95.

Alaska's Weather, Vol. 18, No. 1. Helps readers answer that often-asked question: "What's the weather like?" Also provides glimpses into the ways in which Alaskans cope with their climate. With index; 96 pages, $19.95.

Alaska's Volcanoes, Vol. 18, No. 2. This scientific overview of Alaska's portion of the Ring of Fire brings readers up to date on the activities of the state's dynamic volcanoes. With index; 96 pages, $19.95.

Admiralty Island...Fortress of the Bears, Vol. 18, No. 3. Examines this wilderness/wildlife sanctuary, site of significant mineral wealth and thick forests. With fold-out map and index; 96 pages, $19.95. **LIMITED SUPPLY.**

Unalaska/Dutch Harbor, Vol. 18, No. 4. Commercial heart of the Aleutian Islands, Unalaska and its Port of Dutch Harbor prosper as a gateway to the Aleutians and western Alaska. With index; 96 pages, $19.95.

Skagway: A Legacy of Gold, Vol. 19, No. 1. Jumping off point for the Klondike gold rush, Skagway has seen its fortunes rise, fall and rise again. With index; 96 pages, $19.95.

Alaska: The Great Land, Vol. 19, No. 2. This issue offers an overview of Alaska's six diverse regions, from the islands of Southeast, to the snow-swept Arctic, to the remote Aleutians. With index; 112 pages, $19.95.

Kodiak, Vol. 19, No. 3. One of Alaska's largest communities, fierce wildlife, rugged wilderness and wild waters make up the Kodiak archipelago. With index; 112 pages, $19.95. **LIMITED SUPPLY.**

Alaska's Railroads, Vol. 19, No. 4. This issue looks at the lines that contributed to Alaska's railroad history, and assesses their economic impact on the state. With index; 96 pages, $19.95.

Prince William Sound, Vol. 20, No. 1. This issue looks at the region's resources; its economic hub, Valdez; its people; and its spectacular scenery. With index; 112 pages, $19.95.

Southeast Alaska, Vol. 20, No. 2. Explores the waterways and mountain tops that make up Alaska's scenic Panhandle. Includes a profile of Juneau, Alaska's capital. With fold-out map and index; 128 pages, $19.95.

Arctic National Wildlife Refuge, Vol. 20, No. 3. This issue details the area's natural resources, human use of those resources and the politics that make this remote region so controversial. With index; 96 pages, $19.95.

Alaska's Bears, Vol. 20, No. 4. Details the natural history of Alaska's three species of bears—brown/grizzly, black and polar. With index; 112 pages, $19.95.

The Alaska Peninsula, Vol. 21, No. 1. Active and dormant volcanoes, hidden bays, abundant fish and wildlife and a handful of remote communities characterize the rugged Alaska Peninsula. With index; 96 pages, $19.95.

Kenai Peninsula, Vol. 21, No. 2. This peninsula embraces the traditional Alaska of hunters, fishermen and homesteaders, as well as the modern Alaska fueled by the oil and gas industries. With index; 128 pages, $19.95.

People of Alaska, Vol. 21, No. 3. A chronicle of Alaska's people, from early-day Natives to modern boomers who forge the state's future. With index; 96 pages, $19.95.

Prehistoric Alaska, Vol. 21, No. 4. An up-to-date account of Alaska's land formation, plus the dinosaurs, prehistoric mammals and people who survived here before recorded history. With index; 112 pages, $19.95.

Fairbanks, Vol. 22, No. 1. From its origin as a mining supply depot on the Chena River, Fairbanks has grown into the service and supply center for Alaska's Interior and North. With index; 96 pages, $19.95.

The Aleutian Islands, Vol. 22, No. 2. Details this remote region from the Russians who came more than 250 years ago to today's busy commercial fishing fleets. With fold-out map and index; 112 pages, $19.95.

Rich Earth: Alaska's Mineral Industry, Vol. 22, No. 3. Explores past and present mining in Alaska; from placer and hardrock mining for gold and other minerals to the mining of industrial minerals. With index; $19.95.

World War II in Alaska, Vol. 22, No. 4. An in-depth account of the war in Alaska, including construction of the Alaska Highway, the military buildup and the Japanese invasion of the Aleutians. With index; $19.95.

Anchorage, Vol. 23, No. 1. A comprehensive review of Alaska's largest city: its setting, commerce and transportation, along with its people, culture, recreation and tourism. With index; $21.95.

Native Cultures In Alaska, Vol. 23, No. 2. A look at the traditional lifestyles and rich heritage of Alaska's Native people, including their hopes for the future. With index; $19.95.

The Brooks Range, Vol. 23, No. 3. This issue offers a comprehensive look at the largest mountain range in northern Alaska. With index; $19.95.

Moose, Caribou and Musk Ox, Vol. 23, No. 4. An in-depth exploration of the natural history and life cycles of Alaska's largest ungulates along with traditional uses of the animals. With index; $19.95.

■ ■ ■

To order any of the *ALASKA GEOGRAPHIC®* books listed above, send us your name and address, a list of the books you'd like, and your payment (check or money order in U.S. funds or VISA or MasterCard number and expiration date). Please be sure to add shipping and handling of $2 per book for book rate postage or $4 per book for Priority Mail. Send orders to:

ALASKA GEOGRAPHIC SOCIETY
P.O. Box 93370-MG
Anchorage AK 99509-3370
Phone: (907) 562-0164; Fax: (907) 562-0479

Index